PRAISE FOR

Starved is a come-to-the-table, fill-your-plate invitation to true nourishment. In this run-faster, hustle-for-approval world, this book leads us to a soulful place of connection. Amy Seiffert has written a guide that is at once real and raw, loving and hopeful. Using her own pain and grief, Amy shares with us what she knows to be true: God's amazing grace feeds and renews us.

KAREN JOY HARDWICK, MDIV, MSW
Author of *The Connected Leader: Seven Strategies to Empower Your True Self and Inspire Others*

All of us are hungry for something, but sometimes, without knowing it, we keep desperately filling ourselves with things that won't satisfy. It doesn't have to be this way! With candor, humor, and grace, Amy Seiffert opens up her life and invites us to do the same. Through biblical teaching, practical application, and a keen insight into our human condition, Amy invites us to discover the gifts God has for us that lead to satisfaction and wholeness. If you're worn out and starving for more, pick up this book!

NICOLE UNICE
Author of *The Miracle Moment* and *The Struggle Is Real*

With grace and truth, Amy Seiffert shares how we can authentically hold the tension of releasing control to our powerful God while also taking ownership for ourselves and our community. *Starved* provides practical resources and pathways that empower readers to nourish themselves in sustainable ways. This book is for anyone who has ever felt a little bit "off" yet knows there is so much more to life. Please share this book with everyone you care about!

JENNI WONG CLAYVILLE
Pastor and speaker, National Community Church

Amy Seiffert's book is packed with personal stories that not only resonate with women but also point us back to gospel truth. She offers biblical insight on hot topics in our culture today. I cried, and I smiled. I felt seen, and I felt full.

SIMI JOHN
Speaker and author of *I Am Not: Break Free from Stereotypes and Become the Woman God Made You to Be*

Amy's profound, courageous words will move you to reflect and draw you closer to God. Not only does she provide insightful reflection with each page turn, but she also routinely reminds us that God never intended us to run on fumes!

BETHNY RICKS
Speaker, leadership expert, and author

With humor, vulnerability, and poignant truth, Amy's words will awaken your heart to places you may not have even known needed redemption while leading you into the deeper waters of God's abundant grace and kindness. Her words are refreshing, her challenges are profoundly simple, and the changes she moves you toward are transformational. For anyone who is thirsty for more of God but doesn't know what is missing or how to find it, this book is a gentle guide to experience more of Jesus and become more of who He created you to be!

LINDSEY DENNIS
Author of *Buried Dreams: From Devastating Loss to Unimaginable Hope*

The empty calories of culture aren't cutting it anymore! *Starved* sets a soul-filling table for women who long to feast on God's invitation to freedom and lasting satisfaction for their malnourished souls. Amy serves up *Starved* with a mix of fresh spiritual insights, raw vulnerability, and practical tools that are as easy to use as a fork and spoon.

BARB ROOSE
Speaker and author of *Surrendered: Letting Go and Living like Jesus* and other books and Bible studies

Whenever I eat junk food, I still feel hungry, and I don't feel great either. Spiritually, this applies as well. We are famished for some spiritual nutrition. In *Starved*, Amy delivers a four-course meal of spiritual disciplines that feed our souls. Grab your fork—it's feasting time.

DR. DERWIN L. GRAY
Cofounder and lead elder–pastor of Transformation Church and author of *How to Heal Our Racial Divide: What the Bible Says, and the First Christians Knew, about Racial Reconciliation*

Amy doesn't skirt around difficult topics; she dives right in. With beautiful storytelling, each chapter draws us in, asking hard questions and reflecting on how we are starving our lives. Amy writes with vulnerability and clarity as she chronicles her journey of going from starved to nourished in her personal and spiritual life—and she encourages us to do the same.

FAITTH BROOKS
Author and speaker

STARVED

DEDICATION

For my husband, who gently nods toward the Shepherd's green pastures when I find myself starving.

For my son Robby, whose quiet and courageous leadership brought us all here.

For my daughter, Olive, whose thirst for life will lead her to the Creator of it.

For my son Judah, whose hunger for adventure will lead him to the King of it.

AMY SEIFFERT

STARVED

WHY WE NEED A
SPIRITUAL DIET CHANGE
TO MOVE US FROM TIRED,
ANXIOUS, AND OVERWHELMED
TO FULFILLED, WHOLE,
AND FREE

TYNDALE
MOMENTUM®

A Tyndale nonfiction imprint

Visit Tyndale online at tyndale.com.

Visit Tyndale Momentum online at tyndalemomentum.com.

Visit the author at amyseiffert.com.

Tyndale, Tyndale's quill logo, *Tyndale Momentum*, and the Tyndale Momentum logo are registered trademarks of Tyndale House Ministries. Tyndale Momentum is a nonfiction imprint of Tyndale House Publishers, Carol Stream, Illinois.

Starved: Why We Need a Spiritual Diet Change to Move Us from Tired, Anxious, and Overwhelmed to Fulfilled, Whole, and Free

Designed by Jennifer Phelps

For information about special discounts for bulk purchases, please contact Tyndale House Publishers at csresponse@tyndale.com, or call 1-855-277-9400.

Library of Congress Cataloging-in-Publication Data

A catalog record for this book is available from the Library of Congress.

ISBN 978-1-4964-6029-5 (sc)

Printed in the United States of America

29	28	27	26	25	24	23
7	6	5	4	3	2	1

Hey there! All who are thirsty,

come to the water!

Are you penniless?

Come anyway—buy and eat!

Come, buy your drinks, buy wine and milk.

Buy without money—everything's free!

Why do you spend your money on junk food,

your hard-earned cash on cotton candy?

Listen to me, listen well: Eat only the best,

fill yourself with only the finest.

Pay attention, come close now,

listen carefully to my life-giving, life-nourishing words.

I'm making a lasting covenant commitment with you,

the same that I made with David:

sure, solid, enduring love.

ISAIAH 55:1-4, MSG

CONTENTS

INTRODUCTION

He was eating.

Three years ago, this was the thought I had every single time I looked at my oldest child. The son we'd cried and prayed for through infertile years and monthly personal funerals each time my period arrived. The son named after my husband's late father, who had been killed in the line of duty in 1977 as a Cincinnati police officer. The son who made me a mother for the first time, as two other children followed beautifully behind on the trail he blazed.

The son I didn't want to admit might be sick.

He was eleven now, and he was sleeping more and more during those summer days, but I thought it was just the heat. Heat zaps your energy, right? He would fall asleep in the morning, again in the afternoon, and once again after dinner. And that was after a full night's sleep! Wasn't he growing? I convinced myself his body was just working hard on stretching out his bones. Until he started shivering. If you know anything about Ohio in July, then you know you could fry an egg on the sidewalk and not think anything of it. But there, in the sweltering heat of summer, my once active and playful boy was shivering on a regular basis.

He eventually started spiking fevers, too. That wasn't necessarily abnormal, was it? And then, his stomach started to hurt . . . often. The foods he loved and grew up eating were now causing him nothing but extreme pain and long periods in the bathroom. He started losing weight, and soon, people started noticing.

One too many neighbors started asking me how my son was doing. They mentioned he looked "not quite himself" and "kind of thin." I brushed them off one by one, explaining that he was in a growth spurt like any healthy eleven-year-old boy would be. Kids shoot up quickly and look incredibly skinny in the process. Eventually, they fill back out. My son would fill back out. It was all part of the cycle of growth.

He was fine.

We were fine.

I was fine.

Except we weren't fine. My husband and I started whispering as much to one another at night, staring at the ceiling as we lay in bed and wondering if something was really wrong with our son. If we only whispered it, maybe it wouldn't be loud enough to make it real. But when I looked at my son each morning, shivering and wasting away, I knew it was, in fact, very real.

He was eating, yes, but he was also *starving*.

Like any fierce momma bear woken up to the reality that one of her cubs needs help, I did the only thing I knew to do: I threw myself on the floor of my bedroom and prayed. Well, to be more accurate, I wept. Then, I prayed. I prayed the desperate prayers of a mother unsure how to nourish her child.

I prayed for healing. I prayed for answers. I went so far as to pray for a tapeworm. Of course, I never thought I would pray for one of my children to have a tapeworm; I don't know one single parent that dreams up that kind of reality for their children. But that's where I found myself on that warm autumn morning as I cried on the cream shag rug next to my bed.

I was pleading with God that whatever was stealing weight off of my son's body was something we could solve quickly. As terrible as it may sound, a tapeworm was tangible. It was a temporary problem I thought we could solve, and that seemed better than something like Crohn's disease or some other terrible illness or lifelong disorder.

I didn't know what was wrong. I didn't know what was causing my son to waste away and struggle. I just knew that, before my very eyes, he was starving.

And it was time to figure out why.

Maybe you know what I'm talking about. No, I don't mean that maybe one of your children suddenly started starving without

> We're consuming, we're filling up, we're taking in, but at the end of the day, our souls are still starving.

explanation. I mean that maybe, in one way or another, you're starving too. Truth be told, I think we all are. We're consuming, we're filling up, we're taking in, but at the end of the day, our souls are still starving.

Every day we reach for the things that we believe will enrich our lives. We grab on to the things we think will nourish our souls. We take in what we think will ultimately fill us up. We feast on everything we possibly can, but we're still coming up emotionally and spiritually malnourished.

We're anxious.

We're afraid.

We're overwhelmed.

We're exhausted.

We're longing for more.

We're eating, but we're starving.

And by we, I mean me! I've adopted plenty of practices in my own life in a feeble attempt to feed my own soul. I look to my phone for comfort and security. I tell myself stories to explain away negative feelings or bad choices. I distract and busy myself to avoid dealing with difficult circumstances or hard days. I achieve and achieve and achieve to try to prove my value. I'm filling my proverbial plate with more than enough to feed myself, and yet somehow, I'm still starving for something that will satiate.

Somewhere along the way, we've lost sight of what really nourishes, what really feeds, what really satisfies, what really sustains. In other words, we've lost sight of God Himself—the loving Father who promises to feed us with an everlasting nourishment. Without even realizing it, we've become disconnected from the only source of real, lasting life we have. And because of that, without even realizing it, we're starving.

One New Year's Eve, I was in a hotel room with a few close friends talking over champagne, chocolate, and appetizers. They were telling me about a thirty-day process they were going to start the next day called the Whole30. They were feeling the effects of a holiday season filled with rich foods, buttery baking, and weekly parties, and they wanted to do something to help their bodies feel good again.

Intrigued, I decided to join them. Together, we removed things like gluten, legumes, dairy, and sugar from our diets for thirty days. At the beginning, I braced myself for severe deprivation, but in changing my diet for that month, I discovered something surprising. As it turned out, my body had already been living in a state of deprivation, and this simple change in eating allowed me to actually nourish myself. I had no idea my brain was bothered by sugar, but I felt the mental clarity when I removed it from the equation. I had no clue that dairy irritated my sinuses, but I was breathing easier without it. I didn't realize that grains were making me feel sluggish in the afternoon, but I found a fresh pep in my step without them. I was unaware that what I was eating wasn't actually giving me what I needed until I stopped, looked at what I had been consuming, and chose to make a change.

I think the same can be said for our spiritual diets.

We're told that our brilliant phones are all we need. That real, authentic, face-to-face community isn't that important. That walking with God in the cool of our days isn't where real life is. We're told that politicians and policies will save us. That drowning out our anxiety with news and noise and Netflix will bring peace. That a new leader will mean a better life. We're told that getting that next promotion will be the thing that finally does it. That finding validation in how a man or woman looks at us will complete us once and for all. That building our own comfortable kingdoms with two-car garages and white picket fences will be enough. And worst of all, we believe it. We consume it. We take it all in, again and again and again.

But still, we're starving.

We've been starving ever since the juice dripped down our wrist fresh from the forbidden fruit. Way back in the Garden, Eve had a conversation with the Snake that made her question God's ability to satisfy and nourish her. When the Snake presented her with that shiny, beautiful fruit, he presented with it a question about the God who asked her not to eat it.

Did God really say you can't eat from any tree?

And with that, she began to wonder.

What was it that God actually said?

Why can't I eat from every tree?

Why shouldn't I try this fruit that is clearly good to eat?

Why would God deprive me of something so good for me?

Does He really love me?

Can I trust Him?

Will He take care of me?

Does He want what's best for me?

Should I just take care of myself?

Of course, I'm guessing at Eve's inner dialogue, but it feels like a pretty good guess, as it sounds a lot like my own inner dialogue. I'm guessing maybe it sounds like yours, too. When we're dissatisfied, hungry for more, missing out on substance because we're feeding ourselves with what we think will give us meaning, we begin to question the truth of who God is and whether He can actually fill us up. We begin to question why it is we're starving.

Friends, can I let you in on something I've learned along the way? Our starvation won't cease until we take a good hard look at what we're consuming and commit to making a change. That's what we had to do for my son that summer. It's what I did for my body during that Whole30. And it's what we have to do now if we want to find lasting nourishment for our souls.

> **Our starvation won't cease until we take a good hard look at what we're consuming and commit to making a change.**

What if we took a look at what we actually believed about God and His ability to nourish us? What if we examined the kinds of practices we've developed to feed ourselves in an attempt to discover how they're leaving us spiritually emaciated? What if we looked at our steady spiritual diets and considered some life-giving meal replacements instead? I want us to discover why what we're consuming isn't cutting it, and more importantly, to tap into the source of life that will satisfy and satiate our every hunger: God Himself.

I've walked this road myself, friends. Truth be told, I think I'll keep walking this road the rest of my life. (Thank God for grace, right?) I've been tired of feeling spiritually malnourished all the time, and I've done the digging to get to the bottom of that hunger. Some of it was about what I was taking in. Some of it was about what I was telling myself or allowing others to tell me. Some of it was the way I spent my time looking for quick fixes. Some of it was about what I believed about God, myself, and the world around me. Some of it was linked to how my choices were affecting my nourishment.

I didn't always know what was causing the starvation, but one thing I knew for certain: something needed to change. Just like my son needed a diet change to help his physical body, I needed a diet change to help my soul. I think we all do! And that's what I hope this book will give us: a road map to understanding why we're so malnourished and what we can do to feast on the things that will actually nourish and sustain us.

Because, yes, we're eating, but we're also starving.

And now, it's time to figure out why.

1
PHONE-A-HOLICS UNITE
Starved for Connection

Eight hours and forty-seven minutes.

I didn't know you could even find out that kind of information, but of course you can. If you can find out what the temperature is in Zambia right now or what monkeys are legal in Ohio (lemurs, in fact), you can certainly find out how many hours you're logging daily on your phone. It's called a smartphone for a reason; it knows all.

I made this discovery for myself when a friend told me she was putting limits on her phone use. She was shocked to discover the amount of time she regularly spent on her phone. I encouraged her in this practice but thought it wasn't for me. Surely I wasn't spending that much time on my phone. It was just a few minutes here and there, right?

Well, as it turned out, it was eight hours and forty-seven minutes, to be exact.

Hi, my name is Amy, and I am a phone-a-holic. I'm in recovery, of course, but I'm still an addict. I likely always will be. There's the withdrawal, the shakes, the muscle memory that keeps me reaching for my phone in my pocket when it isn't there because I put it on the countertop during dinner. There's a part of me that will always try to feed myself with whatever I can find behind that phone screen. They say old habits die hard, and I'm here to tell you that, in this case, they're right. It's really hard to let go of something that makes you feel so connected. It's even harder when you don't realize that something is actually disconnecting you from your actual life. From the people right in front of your face. From your own agency. From your soul. From Jesus.

Before this eight-hour-and-forty-seven-minute wake-up call, I had a few phone intervention moments that jarred me awake to the reality of how I was trying to feed myself each time I had that phone in my grip.

There was the time I was answering work emails in the kitchen with one hand and stirring pasta with the other when I faintly heard my youngest trying to tell me something. My preoccupation with dinner and emails was making me annoyed with his need for attention at that moment. Couldn't he see I was working? Didn't he know I had to answer that question right that second? Didn't he understand how important I was? That I was holding up the entire world with this one device? Didn't he know that if I stopped, the world stopped with me?

His little voice finally reached my ears at a shout, "MOM, STOP BEING ON YOUR PHONE BECAUSE I WANT TO SHOW YOU SOMETHING!" This from the kid who doesn't really shout at me. (I have other kids that shout, don't worry.) He had built such a beautiful, stunning Lego dragon, and he proudly wanted to show it to me. I almost missed connecting with my son because I was looking for connection in my phone. That Lego dragon saved the captive princess that evening, even though that princess didn't yet know she needed saving.

Another time, I asked for my family to embark on a fast together for Lent. I asked if the phone owners in our family (only me, my husband, and my son at the time) could put their phones on the countertop for two hours during dinner time. I sensed we were losing the precious evening hours we had for connecting face-to-face to the glowing screens and the illusion of connecting to other people's lives. When I suggested the fast, they looked at me like I had just asked them to give me their left arms, or to lick the trash can, or to use the floor as their plate tonight. It was complete absurdity.

But I couldn't fault them. I was doing the same thing. My desperate desire for connection to my phone was so bad, I found myself searching for my phone on the way to take a shower. Yes, that's right, I needed to take it with me . . . into the shower. Who does that? Somehow, I had gotten to a point where I couldn't be left totally alone to connect with my own thoughts in the quiet of the shower.

See what I mean by addict?

WE'VE GOT A PROBLEM

Enough was enough. I was tired of bowing to my phone. Of needing it like I needed water, or air, or food (or apparently, a shower). I was done with letting this little rectangle tell me what I ought to think about. With letting this little device steal my agency, my time, and my creativity. In one hand-held smartphone, I was looking for every kind of connection I could find, and I was doing it for a whopping eight hours and forty-seven minutes a day.

But when I put it down at the end of the day? When I let my head hit the pillow and my phone was safely charging on the nightstand? Well, friend, I was still starving.

Starving for time with my family.

Starving for authentic and real-life community.

Starving for the kind of connection to God and the people He put in my path that would actually leave me satisfied for the long haul.

Maybe you've been there too. Maybe you've been grabbing on to your phone for dear life, looking to connect with information, with news, with online shopping, with text messages, with emails, with lives on social media. And maybe, like me, you're still starving. Maybe you need to be empowered to let go. To change. To make a switch to your spiritual diet.

If that's you, then let me bless you with this hard-learned

> You can keep scrolling, keep texting, keep posting, and you'll still be starving for the real, lasting connection you hope to find there.

lesson from my own life: you won't find what you're looking for behind the screen of your smartphone. You can keep scrolling, keep texting, keep posting, and you'll still be starving for the real, lasting connection you hope to find there.

And it's not just you and me! It's all of us. We aren't alone in this struggle, friend. According to a study done in 2021, most Americans on average check their phones 344 times every day.[1] *THREE HUNDRED AND FORTY-FOUR TIMES, YOU GUYS!* This is absurdity. This is serious. This is starving us.

The numbers don't lie, friend. The rest of the study went on to show these statistics:

- 71 percent check their phone right after waking up.
- 74 percent feel nervous if they leave their phone at home.
- 35 percent look at (or use) their phone while driving.
- 47 percent are addicted to their phone, by their own admission.
- 53 percent have never gone more than a full day without their phone.
- 48 percent feel panicky when their battery is low.
- 62 percent have their phone by their bed at night.
- 45 percent consider their phone their most valuable possession.

We have a problem, don't we? We're running to our phones to feel better about our lives, but we don't feel that much better when it's all said and done. We're so connected to our phones that we've left little room to connect to anything that matters. Anything that will actually feed and satiate us.

I know because I've been there. I've thought my phone would feed me too. I thought it would bring me life and meet my needs. I believed it so much that I didn't see it was doing the exact opposite. It's a thief, stealing time and connection and the silence and space my soul needs to really live as one loved by God. It's promising nourishment, but it's actually starving me.

A TEMPTATION

What can we do to change that? Beyond just trying in our own strength to put down the phone and find what we're looking for elsewhere, what can we do to ensure we're not starving ourselves with each swipe? How can we feed ourselves with something that will satisfy that deep hunger for connection?

Well, a big part of that is identifying the lies we believe and how we can find true nourishment. After all, our minds are connected to our souls, and our souls are connected to our bodies. Our heads inform our hearts, and our hearts inform our hands. We can't simply change a behavior; we have to change our hearts. And that, friend, is something only God can do.

When Jesus began His ministry, two key things happened that would shape the rest of His time on earth. The first was that He was baptized by His cousin, John the Baptist, in the Jordan River. Immediately, as the text in Matthew says, "The heavens were opened, and he saw the Spirit of God descending as a dove and settling on Him, and behold, a voice from the heavens said, 'This is My beloved Son, with whom I am well pleased'" (3:16-17, NASB). This glorious truth would carry Jesus through every hard and dark moment thereafter: He was beloved. He was loved by God.

It's important for the achievers out there (I'm looking at you, Amy!) to note that up until this point, Jesus had done nothing special. No miracles. No life-changing teachings. No performances to earn accolades. No flipping tables and clearing out religious rhetoric. This was not a title He had earned; this was the identity He was born with.

He was beloved. He was loved plain and simple because He was God's.

Secondly, after His identity was announced, Jesus was led by the Spirit into the desert to be tempted by the devil for forty days and forty nights. Here, the Scripture says Jesus became hungry, which always makes me chuckle. Thank you, Matthew, I was unsure if Jesus was hungry after six weeks of not eating. You cleared that right up for me!

In this obvious hunger, the devil says something important to Jesus: "If you are the Son of God, turn these rocks into piping hot, delicious, satisfying bread. Make this into the finest French baguette you can imagine."

Of course, I'm paraphrasing here, but when I'm hungry, that French baguette is all I want! The point isn't the words themselves, but rather, the temptation behind them.

If you are really who God says you are—if you are His beloved—why would He leave you out here with nothing to eat? I think God is holding out on you. You should just make your own bread and get on with it. Provide for yourself. Get what you need. God can't be trusted. You can do it without Him, and you probably should. Maybe He doesn't love you the way you think He does.

Even though God had clearly, boldly, loudly, and unmistakably declared His love for His Son for all to hear, the devil went after Jesus' belief in that identity. And if the enemy is so bold as to go after the Son of God like that, he will certainly do the same with us. He's questioning Jesus' identity and God's goodness all at the same time. And every single time we turn to our measly phones in an attempt to feed ourselves, the devil is whispering those same questions in our ears too.

Just as Jesus is lured toward the trap of believing He is not loved, so are we. Just as Jesus is tempted to make His own bread, so are we tempted to provide our own nourishment. Just as Jesus was tempted to believe God was holding out on Him, so we are tempted to believe it's up to us. Pastor and Christian leader Russell Moore develops this thought beautifully:

> You will be tempted exactly as Jesus was, because Jesus was being tempted exactly as we are. You will be tempted with consumption, security, and status. You will be tempted to provide for yourself, to protect yourself, and to exalt yourself. And at the core of these three is a common impulse—to cast off the fatherhood of God.[2]

WHAT ARE WE LOOKING FOR?

So, what do we do? How do we deal with these temptations head-on instead of letting them starve us to death? Well, we start by looking to Jesus. There in the desert, His answer to the devil is perfect. "It is written: 'Man shall not live on bread alone'" (Luke 4:4, NIV). This was a truth that Jesus heard all of His life in the Torah. He knew better than anyone that God has better nourishment for us than what we can make on our own. God Himself is the source of our feast. He is indeed the Bread of Life. The only way to be truly satisfied and nourished is to connect with Him, the God who made us and calls us His beloved.

If we know that to be true, it should stop us from trying to find that satisfaction elsewhere. It should stop us from feasting on our phones.

Listen, do I think phones are evil? Of course not! My phone is quite useful in a lot of ways. In fact, I've written 40 percent of my books on my phone while locked in the quiet of my bathroom away from my three amazing and loud

> **The only way to be truly satisfied and nourished is to connect with the God who made us and calls us His beloved.**

children. Phones have the potential to do a lot of good. They let us communicate and connect in a temporal, convenient way. But do I think our phones could be starving our souls? Absolutely. Because each time we pick them up in an effort to feed our need to connect, we're inadvertently cutting ourselves off from an actual connection to the stuff that will satisfy: our people, our community, and ultimately, our God.

The devil deals in the business of lies; it's really his only weapon. One of the lies that he peddles to us about God is that we can't trust Him to provide for us. We can't trust that He will take care of us. That He will provide peace in our anxiety. That He will bring joy in our jails. That He will put hope in place of despair. We can't believe God will actually love us as His beloved children.

And when we don't believe God will provide and care for us as His beloved, we start grabbing for anything we can find to do it ourselves. So much of my need to stay connected to my phone really was because I believed I had to be in charge of everything. If I stopped, I wasn't sure God would provide for me. In all kinds of ways—emotional, financial, spiritual, relational—I looked to my phone to provide what I didn't trust God would.

I think we all do this in some way. We spend hours on Pinterest, trying to put together the perfect outfit or the best mantel so we can feel good about ourselves, but we still end up comparing and complaining at the end of the day. We deep dive into the news so we can stay informed and have some sense of control, but we emerge feeling stressed, doomed, and out of control. We play endless games just to take a break from life, but what we gain is an addiction to the short hits of dopamine that keep us coming back for more. We reach out and text everyone we know when we feel rejected, hoping that salvation will come through validation of any kind (as my pastor likes to say). We judge, like, and shame on our social media platform of choice, only to find it is our own hearts that are more judged, disliked, and shamed in the end. We're looking to provide for ourselves with the smartest tool we have at our fingertips, but in doing so, we're cutting ourselves off from the power of real, lasting connecting with a God who promises to provide all we need.

So, how do we change our steady diet? How do we overcome what may be a downright addiction to feeding ourselves with the connection we hope to find in our phones?

What we need to know is the same thing that Jesus needed to know very early on in His public ministry: you are beloved. When we believe we are God's beloved, we can rest. We can rest from grabbing, from consuming, from entertaining in order to feel loved. We can put down the phone, once and for all.

SITTING IN THE SILENCE

The only way we can really remember and hold on to this truth—this identity we have in God and the belief in His promise to provide—is to feed ourselves by connecting with God. We can't trust God if we don't know Him. We can't rest in what He says about us if we don't make space to listen. And we can't do either of those things without finding consistent connection with God. It's in that space that we'll find what nourishes us.

The practice of silence is one of the ways I recover true connection with God. The first time I was intentional about silence was when I read James Bryan Smith's book, *The Good and Beautiful God*. Smith graciously gives his readers a very simple and small challenge: take five whole minutes in the middle of the day to be silent. Smith isn't trying to make it a miserable five minutes, which I appreciate. He suggests grabbing something warm in a mug, sitting by a window, and being completely quiet.[3]

In theory, this sounded quite lovely. In reality, it wasn't so simple.

I think I spent the first four minutes switching positions on the couch and wrestling my thought monkeys, to-do lists, and grocery items. I was a mess. Why couldn't I stay still and silent? Because I hadn't been practicing it. I was out of silence-shape. I had been feasting on noise and dings and stimulation for so long, my soul had forgotten how to sit still and create space to connect with what would really satisfy.

It was uncomfortable up until that last minute. That last minute was really peaceful. Like a cat finally choosing a nap spot, I settled in to really seeing the green grass, the budding spring trees, and the robins making their afternoon plans. At last I paused to connect with God and His creation around me.

And then my phone alarm went off. (Because of course I had set it to set me free from this excruciating experiment.) My five minutes were up. But it was the first time in a long time that I felt so filled up. I was more peaceful, had found more freedom, and felt more like myself. I didn't feel crabby, anxious, or annoyed. I didn't feel like I was missing out. I felt like the world was okay, even if I rested. In those five minutes, God truly was in control, and I really knew it. Walking away from that silent moment, I knew God would remain in control well beyond those five minutes too. I knew because I'd given myself space to connect with and remember the truth about who He was and who I was in Him.

That's the thing about silence: it's space-making. Silence frees us to listen and to be loved. Silence lets us linger in the goodness of God and to actually practice believing that God will care for us. Silence lets us connect to God. Silence lets us imagine God wrapping His loving arms around us. Silence makes space for the truth to fill the air. Silence brings us the ability to just appreciate the simple beauty in our own back-yard. Silence tells the noise to scram and holds space for God to fill us up as He sees fit.

Silence may feel scary, but it's in that seemingly scary silence that we can find real connection with God. A God who has always worked with soil and gardens, water and fire, mustard seeds and yeast. A God who has whispered in the quiet, who has traveled by a cloud, who has wrestled with our own flesh in the night under the bright, starry sky. A God who has held back seas so that tattered sandals can walk from slavery to freedom. A God who will always take care of us.

I find the space to be silent when I stop starving myself with false connections and start feeding myself with real con-nection to God. It's as simple as that, friend.

Okay, maybe it isn't that simple. I know we all struggle to sit in the silence. I know we struggle to believe God is big enough to take care of us if we're quiet. If we're lonely. If we're afraid. If we're bitter. If we're weak. If we stop checking things off the list. If we take time off. If we stop pushing and proving, answering emails and sending texts. If we're anxious. If we're unproductive.

I know the silence often looms loud for us.

GOD CARES FOR US

But friend, believe me when I tell you there is so much hope to be found in your silence and stillness. There is so much space to connect with and remember the God who will care for you. And I know not just because of the way God has cared for me, but because of the way He has cared for those who have gone before us. Stories fasten the truth to our soul, and I think the stories of the women God has cared for before us can be a comfort to our soul's need to remember. I am a woman, and I love when I see myself in the story. And because of the way women were often thought of in biblical times (as less than, as property, as disposable), it is all the more meaningful to see how God took care of the women who lived then. He took care of everyone—the vulnerable, the weary, the forgotten.

God took care of Jochebed. Who is that, you may be asking? This is Moses' mother. She was a warrior, a hero, a woman filled with faith. And by faith, she put her baby—her tiny, helpless baby—in a basket and sent him down a river. Stop and consider this action for a moment. Jochebed put her baby in the care of the water, believing it had to be better than Pharaoh's grip. And she was right. God honored her amazing faith and restored her son back into her arms (which is one of the best plot twists I have ever read). Moses' story now had a watermark. His very name means "pulled from water." And many years later, Moses had to place his faith in God's waters again, trusting God would hold back the sea so that God's people could find freedom. I don't know for certain, but I like to believe it was the faithful connection his mother had to God that helped spur him on.

God took care of Esther. She was put in an impossible position due to her newly acquired queenship. She became Queen Esther just as an investigation about her people was underway. As news spread that her people, the Jews, were going to be wiped out, she had a choice. Would she trust God and approach the king about her identity? Would she fight for her nation? Or would she remain silent and save herself? You probably know what choice she made. Esther bravely approached the king, and she saved an entire nation. As it turned out, God took care of her.

I could go on and on and on. If I had the pages to do so, I'd tell you every single story of every single woman God cared for along the way.

God took care of Eve.

God took care of Hagar.

God took care of Rahab.

God took care of Hannah.

God took care of Ruth.

God took care of Leah.

God took care of Deborah.

God took care of Mary.

God took care of Martha.

God took care of Lydia.

God took care of Phoebe.

God took care of Junia.

God took care of Chloe.

And those are just the ones we can name! Because as the Bible shows us, God took care of the nameless women too. The bleeding woman, the woman at the well, and the adulterous woman. Each one encountered Jesus. One came by faith, one Jesus sought out, and one had no choice but to face the Messiah. One by one, He took care of them all.

Of course, we know God took care of the men, too. There's David, who God cared for even after so many mistakes and missteps. There's Peter, a member of Jesus' inner circle, who God cared for even after Peter denied knowing Him. And of course, there's Jesus. God's own beloved Son faced ridicule, betrayal, persecution, beatings, crucifixion, and death. But God took care of Jesus. The Father brought victory over death by His Spirit through His Son. God's Son beat death, and Jesus has been next to His Father ever since. God took care of His Son, and in that, He took care of all of us for eternity.

My point? If God was willing, and compassionate, and generous enough to take care of all of these imperfect, sinful, messy people, He will certainly do the same for us.

TRUE CONNECTION

So, if we are going to try to believe this in our hearts, this belief may need some support with our hands. We've got to make a conscious decision to create space to remember this is true. We've got to allow ourselves room to sit in the silence and find real, substantial connection. Maybe it's time to set down our phones and tend to our souls. Maybe, for just a few small minutes at a time, we practice believing God a little more. That God will be our friend when we want to text someone to share our life with. That God will bring us peace when we want to bury our anxiety with pretty pictures and mindless games. That God will fill us with hope when we want to turn to the news to offer a good future. That God will take care of our insecurities when we want to find our confidence in the likes of our social media. That God will feed us with real connection to Him when we're starving for it on our phones.

When I practice replacing my phone with silence, I find true connection. I have felt God's presence and the assurance of being His in the quiet places. I have listened to the best sermons by watching the birds float around my backyard, reminding me that if they have everything they need, then I will, too (see Matthew 10:28-31). I am reminded that I do not need social media likes to make me feel loved and cared for. I do not need my email inbox at zero to feel good about myself (which has happened precisely four times in my life, making it a terrible way to measure my worth). I do not need to be constantly available to everyone. I do not need to be needed. I do not need to look for connection anywhere else than where I am in the presence of God. There, I am loved. I am cared for. I am connected.

There, I am fed.

A Practice

As you look to connect with God, try meditating on the same section of Scripture each morning for a week. Read Psalm 23 very slowly, very intentionally, one word at a time. Leave your phone aside and sit quietly with the truth of God's shepherding and caretaking in your life. Ask God to help you believe Him.

After reading and meditating, choose one word from that Scripture to slowly repeat in your mind for a minute. Then, take that word with you into your day. Let the truth connect you back to Him.

A Prayer

As you breathe, let this prayer flow from you:

Exhale: God, I disconnect from the noise.
Inhale: God, I reconnect with you.

2
CHANGING THE SOUNDTRACK
Starved by Shame

I didn't remember it.

At least not until my son turned eight. That's when a memory unlocked from my own life when I was the same age. This is often the case with trauma. Something horrifying happens, and your brain closes off the memory in order to survive. If you think about it, it's actually quite amazing and also terrible at the same time. Your brain is protecting you from the horrors of what happened until suddenly, something shifts, and it just can't hold it in anymore.

For me, that shift was my son's eighth birthday. It was the key that turned the lock.

In the third grade, a friend in the neighborhood invited me to spend the night. We had fun doing all the normal sleepover things: popcorn, a movie, games. Her older brother was in high school at the time, and I remember thinking it was weird how much time he spent around us that whole night. I didn't really like him. He seemed too invested in us. Too present. Too close. Too much like he wanted something.

In the middle of the night, he sexually abused me.

As my little eight-year-old self walked home that morning, she carried with her all of her sleepover gear in her hands and equal loads of shame in her heart. That little girl made a vow to herself right then and there.

I will not go back over to her house ever again.
I will not set foot in that house.
I will not acknowledge her brother.
I will not talk about this.
The end.

And that was the end for twenty-seven years. Until it all came flooding back on my firstborn's birthday. When I saw his little face, I saw my eight-year-old self in him. I saw the unexplained panic and anxiety that hit me sideways at social events. I saw the way men rounding corners on the sidewalk paralyzed me. I saw it all clearly for the first time in twenty-seven years. The memory had come to the surface, and I had to face the shame.

THE SOUNDTRACK OF SHAME

What are we to do with the shades of shame that accompany our stories? With the shame attached to our own choices or to the choices of others? The shame that is starving us?

The moment I felt the weight of my own shame for the first time since childhood, I didn't know exactly how to deal with it. But I did know this: shame wants to deplete our well-being and keep our souls malnourished. It wants to starve us of the good things that come with vulnerability, honesty, and healing. It wants to lie and lie and lie to us about who we are and what we've done (or in my case, what was done to me) until we believe its voice as truth.

Maybe you know exactly what I'm talking about here. I'd say we all do! Shame has attempted to starve us all in some way. And I don't know about you, but I think it's time we stop giving it the power to feed us what isn't actually nourishing us.

So much research and writing has been done in the past decade about shame. Dr. Brené Brown, a leading voice in this field, has carved a path for us that is so incredibly instructive I cannot possibly do it justice. Her work is monumental. So, let's just leave this one to the expert: "Shame is a focus on self, guilt is a focus on behavior. Shame is 'I *am* bad.' Guilt is 'I did something bad.' . . . Guilt: 'I'm sorry. I made a mistake.' Shame: 'I'm sorry. I *am* a mistake.'"[1]

I love the picture she's painting for us here. It's a picture of the way shame speaks to us. Because whether we realize it or not, shame is talking . . . a lot. Unchecked, it can become the soundtrack to our thoughts, our choices, our identities.

So, my question for us is this: Have you considered the background music playing in your life? The narrative that shame is speaking to you? What stories in your life catch your soul, haunt you, and make you want to hide? What voices have left you anxious, afraid, and cynical? What is shame saying to you to make you feel small?

I think being honest about the soundtrack of shame over our lives is the first step. We can't stop something we don't recognize as wrong, as harmful, as straight up lies. In order to change the music, we have to first acknowledge that we don't like the song already playing on repeat in our minds. We have to call it out for what it is: the soundtrack of our shame. The soundtrack of our starvation.

VULNERABILITY

One of the ways to feed our souls in the face of shame is to name our story—the little moments and the big ones. We need to see our story for what it is, compassionately accept it, and practice being loved through it.

The last sentence was incredibly easy to write, but can I just be honest with you? It's actually incredibly hard to live. Sharing the parts of our stories that we're ashamed of? The parts that have depleted our very being? Well, that's no easy task. But as our friend (I feel like we can call her friend, right?) Dr. Brené Brown says, the remedy to shame is empathy, and the path to empathy is vulnerability. Here's how she puts it: "Vulnerability is the core of shame and fear and our struggle for worthiness, but it appears that it's also the birthplace of joy, of creativity, of belonging, of love."[2]

Sigh.

I wish vulnerability—bringing shame to light—wasn't so critical. But you know who hates light? Our enemy. He loves the dark. He loves to keep us in the dark. He hates to see anything brought into the light because he knows that there we'll find the freedom, the joy, and the healing we so desperately want. In the dark, there is starvation, but in the light, there is nourishment. But we can't get there without a little bit of (okay, a lot of!) vulnerability.

It's so hard to trust other people with ourselves. What if we share the darkest parts of our stories and are rejected? Who can we trust to compassionately hold our pain without shaming us further?

> In the dark, there is starvation, but in the light, there is nourishment.

How do we practice vulnerability with so much on the line?

I want to encourage you with two thoughts that have helped me step out of my own starvation in the darkness of shame. First, trust your spiritual gut. You have intuition on who would be safe to open up to about your struggles. You have a sense of who would be empathetic and careful with your pain. And that's because you have the Spirit of God inside of you. When you ask Him and listen to His leading, you can trust Him to guide you to the right people.

And second, God is your soul-keeper. No one else can feed your soul the way He can. When you choose to share the tender spots in your story, remember that the person on the other end of the conversation does not hold your soul. They may have listening ears, supportive hearts, and empathetic responses, but those things can only encourage toward what's ultimately God's job: the healing of your soul. God is the keeper of your soul. He is the One who holds you. His unfailing love will care for your soul.

Just recently, I felt incredibly threatened and unseen in my office. Eventually, I started to feel cynical toward the person who was making me feel this way. But instead of hiding away and letting shame fester in the darkness, I decided to pay attention. I welcomed cynicism to the emotional table; I brought it out into the light. That's how I was able to realize I needed to say some things out loud. Shame hates when we notice and name what's happening, but vulnerability rejoices there. And this time, I wanted to rejoice with it.

So, I called a friend and aired it all out. She listened. She loved me. She was sad and confused with me. She was a soft landing for my soul. When I hung up the phone, I felt my soul lighten. But when I woke up the next morning, there was still some residue. I still hadn't shaken it all. Friends are amazing, but they aren't magical. Of course, God isn't magic either, but He is powerful, all-powerful in fact. And in that power, God carries things that can heal souls in ways humans alone cannot. I hadn't gotten quiet before God with this situation yet. That morning, I knew I needed my Creator to speak to this part of my soul. So, in the quiet before the day began, I sat with God. And in that space, I sensed the incredible grace He'd given me when I had brought shame on others. Listening to His whispers, I felt a nudge to give grace to the person who was bringing shame to me. I was challenged to do for them what God had so generously done for me.

> **God carries things that can heal souls in ways humans alone cannot.**

Later I spoke to this person and asked for clarity. I bravely told them I was hurt by their comments. Apologies and grace filled the space between us. We listened and learned; we saw each other more fully. We forgave. God took down walls where I wanted to build them. He met me in my pain. He called me out of the starvation of shame and into the nourishment that comes with vulnerability. Just like that, the soundtrack in my mind changed.

AN INVITATION

The beautiful thing about a relationship with God is that He calls us to come to Him. As much as He comes to us, He wants us to choose to come to Him. In our relationship with God, there is a mutual coming. A mutual pursuit. A mutual moving toward one another. God is inviting us to commune with Him, and He wants us to invite Him to commune with us, even in the midst of our shame.

It's an invitation as old as time. We see it happen in the Garden of Eden. There, shame took shape for the very first time. Before the great debacle unfolded, there was a clear statement about who Adam and Eve were: "And the man and his wife were both naked and were not ashamed." (Genesis 2:25).

In the Garden, they were completely free to be themselves. They were unhindered, unashamed, fully confident, alive, and whole. But we know how this story went, don't we? We know about the temptation, the fruit, the fall. We know that with that first bite, shame found its way into the Garden of Eden. And after the fruit was consumed, the starving began.

As their eyes opened to their own nakedness, Adam and Eve felt the need to cover up. One moment they were naked and unashamed, and the next they were hiding and full of shame. The writer of Genesis gives us a glimpse into what happened next: "The LORD God called to the man and said to him, 'Where are you?' And he said, 'I heard the sound of you in the garden, and I was afraid, because I was naked, and I hid myself'" (Genesis 3:9-10).

Just like that, shame entered the Garden gates, strutting in like it owned the place. The result? Hiding, lying, running, and darkness. Adam and Eve hid from their Creator, the One whose good and beautiful image they shared. They feared their Creator, the One who gave them everything they needed. They covered themselves up from their Creator, the One who walked with them in the cool of the day. What a tragedy it is to hide from the One who loves us so!

But we do the same thing, don't we? Thousands of years from that first bite of fruit, we're still running and hiding. We're still afraid and ashamed. In my own life, shame urges me to want to hide from others the way the first couple took leaves and covered themselves up. And more than that, it urges me to hide from God.

Maybe shame urges you in the same way. I'm guessing it probably does. Well, the good news for us, friend, is that we live on the other side of the story. We know how things in the Garden played out. We know what God did when shame entered the story: God came for Adam and Eve. He invited them to come to Him. In their shame, God loved them. And in their hiding, God found them. When everything started to unravel, God started sewing redemption. He made the first animal sacrifice, and He tenderly covered their shame, giving us a hint of the final sacrifice that would nail the weight of shame for all of us forever to the cross.

It seems the story of human history could be summed up in this very same pattern: the shame and hiding of broken humanity is met time and again with the love and rescue of a healing God. Time and again, we're given an invitation out of our shame and into our healing.

COME. EAT. LIVE.

We see this same scene over and over throughout God's story in the Bible. Right in the middle, we hear another invitation from God through the prophet Isaiah:

> *Come, everyone who thirsts,*
> *come to the waters;*
> *and he who has no money,*
> *come, buy and eat!*
> *Come, buy wine and milk*
> *without money and without price.*
> *Why do you spend your money for that which is not bread,*
> *and your labor for that which does not satisfy?*
> *Listen diligently to me, and eat what is good,*
> *and delight yourselves in rich food.*
> *Incline your ear, and come to me;*
> *hear, that your soul may live.*

ISAIAH 55:1-3

Come to Me.

Eat what is good.

So your soul may live.

The Israelites were spending their time and resources on food that didn't satisfy. Sounds familiar, huh? And our God—who doesn't shame but invites with grace—comes for them. He brings with Him an invitation for more.

Come out of your hiding.

Eat what really nourishes your soul.

Live in freedom from shame.

Later, we see this invitation at work in the interactions Jesus had with so many on Earth. For me, the one that resonates the most is the one He had with Zacchaeus, a chief tax collector who grew rich off the extra he demanded for himself. Zacchaeus also happened to be short. This detail matters here because it's what propelled Zacchaeus to climb a tree just to be able to see Jesus.

When Jesus reached the spot where Zacchaeus was hiding, He saw Zacchaeus. And then, He invited Himself over to dinner at Zacchaeus's house. Zacchaeus scrambled down the tree and gladly welcomed Jesus in. Even as gossip rose in the crowd about the audacity of Jesus eating with someone like him, Zacchaeus took the invitation. And what did he get in return? The life everlasting that only Jesus can provide.

Zacchaeus came to Jesus. Jesus offered to dine with Him—to commune with him. And in this sharing of physical food and drink, spiritual nourishment was found. In this moment, Christ helped him overcome his shame, and as a result, Zacchaeus's soul lived (See Luke 19:1-10).

Come.

Eat.

Live.

Finally, we find Jesus Himself taking this very same invitation and shouting it out with all of His might in the temple courts.

> On the last day of the feast, the great day, Jesus stood up and cried out, "If anyone thirsts, let him come to me and drink. Whoever believes in me, as the Scripture has said, 'Out of his heart will flow rivers of living water.'" Now this he said about the Spirit, whom those who believed in him were to receive, for as yet the Spirit had not been given, because Jesus was not yet glorified.
>
> JOHN 7:37-39

Come to Jesus.

Eat and drink what is good.

So your soul may *live* like living water.

Do you see this pattern? It's the original design. God invited us to come into His presence, to eat what is good and nourishing to our souls, and to live in the abundance of freedom and healing that comes with it.

I try to remember this pattern as a practice in my own life. When fear and hiding overtake my heart. When I scream at my kids and regret piles on me for treating them that way. When I judge others' choices and realize my judgment makes me no better. When I step on others to make myself look good. When shame threatens to starve me from the nourishment I need.

Then, I come to Jesus any which way I can.

Sometimes it's in my bathroom because life is loud out there, but in here, I can lock the door and be alone. Sometimes I get up early while it's still quiet and close my eyes, imagining a huge feast in front of me with Jesus at the table. He is smiling, eagerly waving me over and pulling out a chair for me to join Him. And sometimes, when shame threatens to keep me from the table, Jesus pulls me in. He embraces me with all the love and grace I need to remember that I am welcomed, I am whole, and I am healed because I'm with Him.

In truth, this often feels like a practice of resistance. I am resisting the plight of Adam and Eve. I am resisting an enemy who loves to keep me in the dark and hold me hidden in my shame. I am resisting the ancient path. And instead, I'm accepting an invitation as old as time. I'm embracing the way of love. I'm coming out of hiding, leaving fear at the door, and letting Jesus' love cover my shame.

I am coming.

I am eating.

I am living.

Part of my healing process from the past abuse was coming to Jesus and finding nourishment in His presence. I came to a counselor who tenderly spoke truth and light. I came to my closest friends and shared what had happened.

I practiced eating what was good. I listened to worship music. I poured out my heart to God. I surrounded myself with compassionate people. I took slow walks in the woods. I asked the really hard questions about where God had been in that moment and wrestled with the silence, fear, and abandonment that surfaced with these memories.

Believe it or not, being vulnerable and deeply honest is good food for the soul. Because now, I am living. I am able to laugh, to fall down, and to stand back up. I'm able to extend forgiveness and to be forgiven. I have opened up the parts of me that I thought were bad—my desires, my beauty, and my body—and I am living more freely with these God-given gifts.

On the days I don't take care of my soul very well, it's easy to believe the soundtrack shame speaks over me. That I am unlovable, stupid, irresponsible, rejected, unacceptable, and bad. But years of counseling, antidepressants, community, and Jesus Himself have taught me otherwise. They've called me into the light and into the truth.

I am loved, even with my scars.

I am delightful, even as a sexual abuse survivor.

I am God's masterpiece, even though my body felt broken during infertility.

I am wanted, even when my mental health suffers and tells me otherwise.

I am beautiful, even when I feel like I'm not.

Oh friend, as we keep traveling together toward a well-fed soul, may we notice and name the lies in our own stories. May we acknowledge our shame and call it out into the light. May we choose vulnerability. May we accept the invitation from our loving Father. May we bring our full selves to His full banquet. And may we allow God to replace our shame with His grace.

A Practice

Set aside some time by yourself this week to bring your shame into the light. Find a private place without distraction or noise. Ask God to meet you there. And then, share your shame with your Father. If you like to journal, write it out. If you're a verbal processor, talk quietly with God. Whatever helps you express yourself to Him, try that as an avenue to share your shame with the Lord. Then, ask Him to lead you toward a healthy next step. Should you share your story with someone safe and empathetic? Should you seek professional support or wise counsel? Ask the Spirit to lead you toward the freedom and nourishment you can find in being vulnerable.

A Prayer

Close your eyes and hold your palms open, facing down. This posture from Richard Foster helps us as we release our fears and receive God's truth and peace. In this position, pray to the Lord, naming what is making you anxious, annoyed, or afraid. Confess what shame is trying to keep you hidden from God. Imagine yourself dropping your burdens and making room for grace to fill your hands instead.

Then, turn your palms up, ready to receive God's grace and love. Thank God for the invitation to come, to eat, to live. Sit in the truth that your Father will always welcome you with grace, compassion, and love. In His light, there is healing.

3
HUMBLE PIE, ANYONE?
Starved for Humility

Humble pie is a regular meal around here.

Truth be told, I'd rather not have it served up so often, but time and again I find it waiting for me on the other end of some not-so-humble moments.

Recently, one of my very creative and innovative children decided to take on a Perler bead creation. If you don't already know, let me just inform you of the fact that Perler beads are from the devil. These tiny and deceivingly innocent colorful plastic pieces slide on top of plastic grids to make designs that melt into one cohesive art piece. Users, beware! If you're carrying your child's Perler creation—equal parts fragile and precious—to the ironing board and just so happen to bump into anything at all? Game over! You will find yourself contending with rivers of tears and scattered beads for hours. You will find these melted beads in your carpet, in your hair, down your shirt, and generally in the most unimaginable places . . . for days. Perler pro tip: bring the iron to the creation instead of the creation to the iron! Consider yourself warned.

This particular day, my child decided to take the melting matters into her own hands. She took her mosaic upstairs, got out the iron, plugged it in, let it heat up, and melted her creation together. Being a good citizen, she wanted to put the iron away when she was done. Because everything has a home around here (as she has been rightly taught), she knew exactly what needed to be done to put things away and back in order. With the best of intentions, she unplugged the piping hot iron and promptly set it face down in the cute teal plastic bin where it lives, on a wooden shelf in our laundry room. Then, she walked away.

Not long after, I smelled hot, burning plastic throughout the house. It was a scent reminiscent of the time I tried to curl my Barbie's long blonde hair, and it was foul, you guys. Following the scent, I came upon the iron and went to pick it up. However, when I did, the plastic bin came right with it. Holy matrimony had occurred, and these two had become one. Finally prying the iron free with some elbow grease, I stared at the hole left in its place: a perfectly shaped iron silhouette. And the iron? Oh, it was covered in melted plastic.

Like any parent, I immediately went to my daughter for an explanation. We had a long talk about taking care of hot things, being responsible, and generally trying not to burn the house down. I carefully explained to her the importance of being careful, of asking for help, of paying attention, and then I went on my way, silently patting myself on the back for this parenting fail turned parenting lesson.

Less than a week later, I was in the kitchen starting the process of making yogurt for my son. (Yes, we make our own yogurt. Yes, it's a staple of my son's diet. Yes, I'd rather buy it. Yes, this is where we are.) The yogurt-making process isn't simple. It involves slowly heating up a half gallon of milk to 180 degrees in a big pot on the stove. On this day, as I put the milk on the burner, my oldest son came down ready for soccer practice. I was the shuttle for my kiddos that night, so we quickly loaded up in the car and headed to the first stop of several to drop off and pick up kids from their various activities.

Of course, I forgot the yogurt. I left the milk in its pot, simmering on medium-high heat. This is standard ADHD life for me. Zipping around, getting a million things done at once, and forsaking the previous task for the next one. Some days, I am way more focused. Other days, not so much. This day, as it turned out, was not so much.

After soccer drop-off, I popped into the grocery store to grab a few items on my list. I then sauntered down the gluten-free snack aisle. There, I also remembered my son's need for a bike lock, so I took a left turn and walked across the store to grab one. And finally, a full forty-five minutes later, I went home.

There's nothing quite like walking in the door to the smell of sour, burned milk. The milk had simmered down to a cara-melly substance, the pot was charred, and the kitchen was terribly hazy. What was also not spared in the aftermath? My pride. Hadn't I just given a riveting sermon on leaving piping hot items unattended in our home? Hadn't I just passionately instructed my daughter to remember not to burn the house down? Hadn't I just talked in detail about the importance of paying attention in using anything hot?

Yes, I had. And yet here I was, the pot calling the kettle black. Literally! Pride comes before the fall, after all. Here's another slice of humble pie, Amy!

A CELEBRATION OF HUMILITY

Confession: humility isn't easy for me. (Not so shocking, huh?) Besides the obvious, I think that's because I used to think humility meant something negative. I thought that in order to be humble, I had to demean myself in some way. That humility involved emotional self-flagellation and deprecation. That it was about making sure I saw myself as the worst of the worst. That it required me to deflect all praise and ward off any compliments. After all, wasn't I just a worthless, rotten, dirty sinner?

A wise friend reminded me of the truth about humility while we were on a walk in the woods. As she pushed a stroller under the tall and mighty oaks, she talked about how often we forget that we are made in God's good and glorious image. We bear the image of God, a strong and secure God, a beautiful and brave God. We are God's reflection. We carry within us a resemblance to Him. And because of that alone, our dignity, value, and worth as God's image-bearers give us a glorious and weighty thing to carry. Humility—real humility—doesn't ask us to disregard or downplay those things. Instead, it allows us to celebrate them.

Graciously receiving a compliment is a beautiful practice as an image-bearer of the King. Standing confident, head held high in strength and dignity, laughing at the days to come? This is the description of the woman in Proverbs 31:25 who trusts in God. Fighting for things like equivalency in honor, pay, rights, and position for every single human is not prideful. In fact, it points right at the inherent worth we have as image-bearers. It's humility that allows us to recognize we've been given an incredible gift as these image-bearers, and it is a gift worth celebrating.

My friend gave me an important lesson in the real meaning of humility that day. I hope her reminders bring the same to you. We aren't called to demean our dignity in the name of humility. Humility isn't about humans feeling worthless; humility is about recognizing the matchless worth of God Himself. Together, may we deconstruct any dangerous form of pride that threatens to starve us from the true and beautiful gift of real humility that God gave to us and Jesus models for us. May we celebrate the humility that will feed us well!

> Humility isn't about humans feeling worthless; humility is about elevating the matchless worth of God Himself.

THINKING OF YOURSELF LESS

In an effort to embrace the gift of humility, I did some digging to discover more about it. In that digging, I found one of the best definitions I've seen on humility: "This is true humility:

not thinking less of ourselves but thinking of ourselves *less*."[1] This really is it, isn't it? The simple truth about pride is that it keeps our eyes focused on ourselves, and that's one of the fastest ways to starve. I know because it's starved me more than a few times. Sure, this maneuvering around the world to make sure it's all about me and getting what I want might feed me for a little while. In those seasons, I tend to operate as if life is like one of those polite but cunning grocery store game shows where my only objective is to get as much as I can in my cart. Every woman for herself out here! But when the horn blows and the game stops? When my cart is full and my soul is empty?

Then, I'm left starving.

Thinking less about myself is the answer. It's the start of feeding myself with the right things—the things that nourish. But you guys, it's not easy for me to do. I struggle not to put myself first all the time in my own world. It happens when I am in a situation where my soul wants to make sure it gets the credit and recognition it deserves. You'd think this would occur mostly in critical moments with a lot on the line, but trust me, it happens in even the tiniest of situations where I feel I'm missing out on what I'm owed. Like the time friends thanked someone else for the amazing recommendation of a book, even though I was the one who made the suggestion. No, I didn't even write that book, but my soul wants to reach out for the credit as much as Eve wanted to grab that shiny fruit in Eden. Would I really be nourished if I was fed what I was looking for? Hardly. Sure, I may get the recognition, but I wouldn't find life.

It happens when I choose self-sufficiency, trying to cram one more email in while making dinner and believing I can juggle all the balls in the air. I don't need to trust God with getting everything done because I can do it myself. Or when I pursue self-promotion, making sure everyone knows how much work I've done and how great of a job I did in getting all that work done. Or when self-indulgence is my goal and I watch, eat, drink, purchase, and take for myself what I want, when I want.

The common denominator here? Self! Feeding on the world of self is sucking the life from us. Thinking only about ourselves is cutting us off from real, lasting nourishment. And it's a practice born out of pride, which may be one of the sneakiest things to detect in our lives. It's so intricately woven into everything, it's difficult to even pull at the threads to find the source. But as pride threatens to starve so many parts of who we are, it's imperative to our nourishment that we begin to root it out.

One of the best ways to uncover pride is to look for the places in my life where I am thinking primarily of myself. In those places and spaces I think I can handle it all on my own? Where I'm worried about what I want and need more than anything? Where I'm concerned with myself above all else? That's where pride takes root in me, and if it's left there to grow, it can create one of the biggest foes to living a spiritually nourished life.

The good news? Humility—thinking less of self—is the friend that can pull us back to reality.

COME AND BELIEVE

So if pride is starving us and humility will help us find nourishment, what can we feast on to help us as we go? I think our food can be found in one of the most beautiful names Jesus calls Himself: the Bread of Life.

Jesus says, "I am the bread of life. Whoever comes to me will never go hungry, and whoever believes in me will never be thirsty" (John 6:35, NIV). What an equally stunning and confusing statement! In the greater context, this is followed by more stunning and confusing language about eating Jesus' body and drinking His blood. Sounds absurd at first glance, right?

Truth be told, this was a hard teaching even then. Many stopped following Jesus when they heard it because they simply couldn't understand what He meant. To keep us from meeting the same fate, I want to take a closer look at this passage together.

Jesus uses two words that help me simplify this profound moment: *come* and *believe*.

When we regularly practice coming to Jesus, He will meet our needs. I know because I've experienced it. I have found deep peace, hope, and rest in His presence. And I've found it not just by coming to Him, but by believing He will satisfy every need and quiet every worry when I do. But to get there, we have to lay down our pride. We have to embrace the humility that asks us to acknowledge our need for Jesus. We must come and believe, and we must do it with humility.

Is it always easy to lay down our pride, even in the presence of God? Certainly not! The hard truth about pride is that it wants to dethrone God and make me queen instead. In my most natural, unredeemed state I am crowning myself queen, grabbing my scepter, and making everything about me. When I find myself annoyed because that position is threatened, that is my pride at work. It's my natural state—the one that serves my flesh and doesn't want to need God.

For me, this is the sneakiest part of the struggle: the not-needing-God part. I am on staff at my church, speak and teach God's Word, and write books about what I've learned through Him. Of course I need God! Except when I don't. It's funny how much I feel the need for God Monday morning through Thursday evening. But once I reach the weekends? Suddenly, I don't feel nearly as desperate for His leadership and grace in my life. I'll take it from here, God. Thanks for helping me through the mundane and overwhelming daily grind, but now I've got it covered. Pass me the crown, because I'm in charge of filling up my own soul on whatever I'd like until Monday morning at least.

Underneath this way of thinking isn't just a pride that tells me I can rule my life just fine; there's also hidden with it a belief about who God really is. Maybe God doesn't want to join us in our joy. Maybe God isn't into laughter and adventures and fun. Maybe God is not the giver of all good gifts. Maybe God isn't really enough.

This is where those two words—come and believe—become vital. Jesus is the Bread of Life! And He is inviting us to be nourished, fully and deeply, by coming and believing. It's a generous invitation that warms the coldest heart. We are invited to clap praises with the oaks, stand in awe with the sunsets, be healed by the sea. To add chairs to our tables for other humble and broken people. To share in the storytelling and laughter, the shared food and experiences, the hope and healing. This is not a stingy Bread of Life we are dealing with here. Jesus is the Bread that offers third helpings, gives full bellies, and then has twelve baskets of leftovers just as good as the first bite. When we come and believe with humility—when we allow ourselves to know and experience who He really is—we'll find life.

THE HUMILITY OF A KING

The truth is, sometimes we're starving for humility because we simply don't want to put down the crown. But when we consider who God is—and I mean who He *really* is—it makes His greatness and our smallness not something to fear, but something to love.

I love Sue Bohlin's thoughts on this. She writes:

> We don't look at the sun and say, "How arrogant of it to shine so brightly, to relentlessly give off heat and light that makes life possible on the earth." It's the nature of gargantuan balls of burning gas to do these things. Our response to the sun is one of respect, gratitude and fear: we can't even look directly at it for more than a glance or it damages our eyes.
>
> It's not arrogant or prideful for God to shine with a radiance beyond a million suns. That's what glory does: it radiates. It shines. That's how He is, that's who He is. . . .

The only response to that kind of God that makes any sense is to fall down at His feet and worship Him.[2]

Along with such beautiful and blinding glory, He is also the King of all creation. That means He is worthy of our praise, our devotion, and our lives. If God really is who He says He is—all powerful, all knowing, self-sufficient, completely holy, always pure, fully right, infinitely good, completely loving—then the only possible response would be to worship Him with the adoration and humility He deserves.

> The epitome of humility is the day Heaven became human.

Which is why the most stunning and shocking move the almighty and all-powerful God ever made was to disrobe from His glory, step out of the beauty and majesty of Heaven, and become like one of His created beings. Why? So that He could bring us back to Himself. The epitome of humility is the day Heaven became human. Jesus took on flesh to serve and suffer at the hands of His own creation so He could save us from our sin. He saw the ocean of despair we could not possibly cross, and He crossed it on our behalf.

He chose humility—a humility fit for a King.

I am so very drawn to the oxymoron of a humble God. What tale of any of the gods has ever included a humble one? Our God is the only one.

This humility is so beautifully described in Philippians:

Do nothing from selfish ambition or conceit, but in humility count others more significant than yourselves. Let each of you look not only to his own interests, but also to the interests of others. Have this mind among yourselves, which is yours in Christ Jesus, who, though he was in the form of God, did not count equality with God a thing to be grasped, but emptied himself, by taking the form of a servant, being born in the likeness of men. And being found in human form, he humbled himself by becoming obedient to the point of death, even death on a cross.

PHILIPPIANS 2:3-8

Let's pay attention to the verbs above (yes, we're still dissecting grammar here, people). They give us so much insight into what Jesus thought, what He felt, and what He did.

He did not *count* His equality.

He did not *grasp* His deity.

He *emptied* Himself.

He *took* the form of a servant.

He was *born* like us, human.

He *humbled* Himself.

He *obeyed* to the point of death . . . on a cross.

And what happened as a result?

Therefore God has highly exalted him and bestowed on him the name that is above every name, so that at the name of Jesus every knee should bow, in heaven and on earth and under the earth, and every tongue

confess that Jesus Christ is Lord, to the glory of God
the Father.

PHILIPPIANS 2:9-11

The Father highly *exalted* Him.
The Father *bestowed* on Him the name above every name.
The Father *bestowed* a name that all will bow to.
The Father *bestowed* a name that every tongue will confess.
In short, Jesus' humility brought the gifts of God's goodness. And the same is true for us! When we choose humility, we're choosing the path that leads to every good and perfect gift God wants to give us. We're trading our scraps for the full nourishment of the Bread of Life.

THE PRACTICE OF LAYING DOWN OUR PRIDE

We all want to be fed. We want to be nourished. We want to find the fulfillment that comes with embracing our humility. But how do we actually get there? How do we step into the practice of laying down our pride—our need to be superior— and practice picking up humility—our need for the Superior?

We practice worshipping God, not ourselves.

Author C. J. Mahaney offers many purposeful suggestions on worshipping God in his amazing little book *Humility: True Greatness.*[3] I have adapted three of them, and they have been very helpful to me:

1. *Admit your daily dependence on God.* For me, this often comes with a physical posture of humility to mirror the

desired posture of my heart. Typically, I spend this time on my knees. This isn't something I do for hours; it's usually just a few minutes. But in this position, I refuse to hide my weaknesses, my fears, my anxieties, and my sins. I humbly come and lay it all before the throne of grace. Maybe I simply name each heavy thing. Maybe I just bow my head and acknowledge my humanity and Jesus' divinity. Maybe I take a walk and worship God, casting my cares on Him. There are so many ways to admit our needs to our good and gracious Father. There are so many ways to declare our dependence on Him. And the gift we will find when we do? A greater humility and a greater grace.

2. *Consider Calvary often.* Pastor Tim Keller has taught that there are only two ways to fulfill any law: to obey it or to pay it.[4] So it is when it comes to the law God laid out for us with Moses. Someone had to pay it, and that's exactly what happened at Calvary. Jesus not only lived the law perfectly here on Earth, He paid for it fully with His work on the Cross. What a good Father we have to create a plan to pay for mistakes and offer us redemption! How can we be prideful when we consider Calvary as often as we can? To consider the Cross often is to worship the King, and in that practice, we find humility.

3. *Practice thanksgiving.* G. K. Chesterton once said, "The worst moment for an atheist is when he is really thankful and has no one to thank." This is God, the maker

of every good and perfect gift. The maker of us! The giver of our talents, our treasures, and our time here on Earth. Giving thanks to God can only happen when we embrace humility. When we recognize that we are not the makers of ourselves. God is. With that in mind, may we practice thanksgiving for all that we are filled up and satisfied with from the hand and heart of God.

Thinking on humility often calls to mind wisdom from Proverbs: "God, I'm asking for two things before I die; don't refuse me—banish lies from my lips and liars from my presence. Give me enough food to live on, neither too much nor too little. If I'm too full, I might get independent, saying, 'God? Who needs him?' If I'm poor, I might steal and dishonor the name of my God" (Proverbs 30:9, MSG).

Some versions suggest that if we get too full, we might "forget God" (CEV).

Friends, this is my prayer for us today. May we not feast so much on our self-sufficiency that we forget our great and daily need for our good Father. May we not be so prideful that we decide we are superior to our own Creator. May we not worship ourselves but worship God. May we never devalue ourselves but elevate the true and rightful King.

A Practice

Take a few minutes to admit your dependence on God. If you are able, kneel in prayer. Then consider the Cross and what Jesus did to win you back. Consider what it meant for Jesus to leave paradise, clothe Himself in skin, and be abandoned, rejected, beaten, and crucified. And then finally, practice giving thanks to God. Show Him gratitude for who He is and all you have in Him. Ask Him to help you be nourished by humility.

A Prayer

As you breathe, let this prayer flow from you.

Inhale: God, I want less of me.

Exhale: God, I need more of You.

4

PRAYING POLITICS

Starved for a King

"I found myself praying to . . ." And then she said a politician's name.

This quiet admission came from a friend over hot coffee and perfectly crumbling muffins. We were in the corner of one of our favorite coffee shops, surrounded by people ordering drinks, chatting, and laughing when her whispered confession cut through the noise. The moment she said it, my eyes widened; I may have even choked on my muffin! Did she really just say that?! She just admitted to replacing Jesus with a political candidate in her prayers. That cannot be right, right?

Though outwardly I appeared stunned by her admission, inwardly I was almost relieved by it. My eyes widened as she spoke because her confession might as well have been my own.

My own heart had been found out. While I may not have voiced it the same way, I had done the same thing. In the early days of 2020, I was putting my hope in the kingdom of a potential president, not the Kingdom of God.

We didn't intend to talk politics that day. We had actually met to discuss the book of Matthew together. But as the gospel lay flat in front of us, we laid ourselves bare before it. We both had big, big feelings about white evangelical Christians bonding with right-wing extremism. We had fears, opinions, and judgments about the pending election. We had huge hopes for the future of our country. By themselves, there's nothing wrong with those things. On their own, they aren't cause for starvation.

But when they become our world? Our kingdom? Then, we're starving before we even realize it.

My friend's confession that day helped me see my own need to do the same. I had not been honest with myself about whose kingdom I was trusting in at the moment. I had not opened myself up to God about it. I had not asked what the Spirit of God might have to say about my politics bonding to my faith in a very real way.

I had not known I was starving.

OVERTHROWING THE KING

So much ink has been spilled on the relationship between politics and religion. News stories, blogs, articles online, social media posts—it seems like every detail of the church's relationship to politics has been covered somewhere. There's a lot to work out through pen and paper and heart and head.

What's interesting to me is that, if we pull back the curtain a few thousand years, we see the very same problem. In the pages of the Old Testament, we find a group of men among God's people who decided that they no longer wanted God as their King. They wanted a worldly king instead, like all the other nations around them. We can find all the details about how it played out in the book of 1 Samuel.

Samuel was the God-appointed prophet, priest, and judge for the Israelites at that time in history. After the Israelite elders requested an earthly king, Samuel let them know he considered this to be a really bad idea. He wanted to stop them from making such a huge mistake, but God? God told Samuel to let the people have their king. Let them have their choice and see if it's really what they want. Let them feed themselves with what they think will satisfy.

But along with this command, God made one thing very clear: if God's people chose a worldly king, they were making a choice to reject God as their King. Having both? Two kings—the Almighty God and one whose heart was after his own kingdom of prestige, power, and possessions? That just wasn't an option.

Just as Samuel suspected, this choice to have a king—like all the other nations—proved to be a poor one for the Israelites. King after king built a name for himself, erected idols for the people to worship, and ultimately forgot God was in the picture at all. These kings—who were not after God's own heart—were allured by power, prestige, and pleasure. They worshiped other gods and made a mess of the kingdom. It got ugly over and over, leaving bloodstains and bruises every-where, until there was nothing but corruption in the kingdom.

It would be easy to read these events with an air of judgment. As much as I'd like to say, "I would never willingly let someone overthrow God as King in my life," I think we know we run the risk of doing the same today. We might already be doing it—starving for a King while cutting ourselves off from the only One who deserves the throne. As I think about the political landscape of the Israelites who rejected God as King, I see so much of our current landscape in the American church and in my very own heart. Because I resonated with what my friend shared in the coffee shop that morning. I was no better than these Israelites. I'd opted for a worldly king to save our nation and in doing so, had overthrown God as King over us all.

A HEART CHANGE

On January 6, 2021, as I watched Trump flags fly next to wooden crosses and statements boasting "Jesus Is Lord" and "Trump for President" sewn on the very same fabric, I felt utter grief and confusion. It's one thing to believe these two things at the same time. It's another when the beliefs seem to be one and the same. This was Christian nationalism at its finest hour. A political party was fused to faith, and the result was a multifaceted riot. For the church, overthrowing Jesus as King and replacing Him with a president was the biggest insurrection of all. As a church—as a body of believers—we were devouring each other in the name of politics.

This is what happens when we overthrow Jesus as King of His people.

But friend, let me be very clear. I was doing the very same thing. I was putting all of my trust in a new president and a new administration. I wanted them to save us. To change us. To bring hope and healing. To bring good news. I may not have had flags on the steps of the Capitol, but I am not exempt from the rebellion that was happening in my own heart. I am just as much to blame for taking Jesus off the throne and replacing Him with a new political party as anyone else.

In many ways, we all are. This one isn't on just one political party or denomination or belief system. It's on all of us.

My pastor shared a great sermon in that season about how we cannot legislate heart change. That's an inside job—a Holy Spirit job. The problem we're running into is that we're looking for outside rulers to do an inside job. No political party can save us from our sinful hearts. No leader can feed us in a way that will satisfy. And if we don't want to remain in starvation, we have to let the Spirit of the one true King work in us to change our hearts.

> The problem we're running into is that we're looking for outside rulers to do an inside job.

I absolutely believe the gospel will cause policy change. In fact, I believe that it must. Continued hard work must be done against white supremacy, discrimination in the criminal justice system, the oppression of non-white communities, and the pay gap. We must advocate for women's rights, equal rights and opportunity, true justice for the marginalized, and care for the widows and the orphans. Systems must be changed, and it is imperative that followers of Jesus be involved in making those changes happen. But in order for the gospel to change our systems, our policies, and our nation for the better, we as Christians have to allow our hearts to be changed for the better first.

The moment we put our actual faith in presidents and policy change to save us—the moment we tether our hearts to a political party—they will fail us. Yes, each political party has some good policies and ideals. And each of us may gravitate toward a different party based on what value of God's Kingdom we hold dear. But the way our politics have overthrown the one true King? It's dividing us. It's hurting us. It's starving us.

We are Christ followers, first.

We are brothers and sisters in Christ, first.

We are citizens of heaven, first.

We are sons and daughters of the Most High King, first.

We starve when any other identity marker is first.

STUFFED, BUT STARVING

During the 2020 election cycle, I consumed copious amounts of news and media. I was taking it in on every platform, every station, and every conversation. But as it turned out, all that consumption didn't satisfy my hunger. It left me tired, irritated, anxious, and afraid. Interestingly, physical and spiritual malnourishment feel similar. This is about the same way I feel after a Big Mac, French fries, a milkshake, and an apple pie.

I was stuffed, but starving. And if I wanted to be nourished, I realized quickly that something would have to change.

In the article titled, "Jesus Is Not a Republican and Christianity Is Not Nationalism," Zachary Wagner writes:

Christianity is not nationalism. . . . Christians should not be afraid of what will happen to the United States. As Christians, we have renounced our citizenship to this nation in favor of our citizenship in God's kingdom (Phil 3:20). This means that I have more in common with a Christian woman in Nigeria with whom I am bonded by the blood of Christ than I have in common with my co-citizens of the United States. Because of this, my hope is not built on the future and flourishing of America. Christians should seek and serve the good of our nation and its institutions as we are able. God told his people during the Babylonian exile, "Seek the prosperity of the city to which I have sent you as exiles" (Jer 29:7). But seeking the prosperity of our nation does not make us Americans in an ultimate sense any more than seeking the prosperity of Babylon made the Jewish exiles Babylonian. We are Christians first, Americans second. If loyalty to American identity compromises our allegiance to Christ, then let us reject our American identity without hesitation.[1]

We have more in common with a woman in Nigeria who is a sister in Christ—who is family—than we do with many of our co-citizens of the United States. We both have the same good, adoring, mighty Father. She is my sister, and that surpasses all other allegiances. This profound and freeing truth watered my thirsty soul. When I read this article, I sighed with relief. I felt very free to say: I may feel politically homeless, but

I am a citizen of heaven. And I will do my best to lay down my vote for others.

We ought to feel the complexity of the polarized American political system if Jesus is King. No one political party fully lines up with the culture of King Jesus. I am pro–Black lives mattering, pro-life, pro–women being treated equally, pro–services to the underserved, pro-kindness, pro-Jesus. Somehow those things seem like they cannot line up on a ticket, and it's maddening. It's polarizing. It's tearing the church apart.

I love the way Tony Robbins puts it: "Change happens when the pain of staying the same is greater than the pain of change." In other words, change happens when starvation has set in. When the persistent hunger makes us increasingly uncomfortable. When we're no longer satisfied with being stuffed but starving. When enough is finally enough.

Friends, if we want to avoid feeling stuffed and starving here, then I'd argue it's time for a change in what we're consuming. Our souls need a pantry sweep. We need to take out the additives, the extras, the sneaky maltodextrin and starches that we had no idea were even in our soul-spices. Like preservatives, lies have slipped into our faith and slowly made us afraid.

If this person is president, the world will burn.

If this policy is in place, we will never recover.

If our freedoms are taken, the church will die.

But the last time I checked, we serve a King who is bigger than any fear, any lie, any political party, and any president. If God is King, we need not fear. His Kingdom holds us and leads us and guides us and keeps us. And if that's true, why are we allowing ourselves to consume things that want to convince us otherwise?

Fear through political rhetoric has found its way into the pantry of our souls, but fear isn't an ingredient that will nourish. In fact, it's never an ingredient given from God. Take a look at how Timothy reminds us: "God has not given us a spirit of fear, but one of power, love, and sound judgment" (2 Timothy 1:7, CSB).

A spirit of power, love, and sound judgment—those are the ingredients for nourishing our soul. Fear starves our soul, but the gifts of God's Spirit feed it. If we want to be fed—really and truly fed—then we have to consume less fear and more power, love, and sound judgment. We have to put down our phones, our newspapers, our social media feeds, our chosen news station, our political parties, and every other thing that's stoking the fear that leaves us stuffed but starving. We have to stop serving a king and a kingdom that won't satisfy in order to make space for the only One who will.

This may take some soul searching on our part, but the discovery is worth the deconstruction. It is worth taking language, thoughts, and assumptions captive, examining them and deciding whether they ought to stay or go. Do the things we're consuming and putting our hope in on a regular basis line up with the King we want to serve? If they don't, then they've got to go. I know this won't be easy. In fact, I know we'll get it wrong at times. But friend, it is worth the confessing, repenting, and lamenting where you have overthrown Jesus as King. It's worth it because it creates space to place Him back upon His rightful throne in your life.

THE TRUE KING AND HIS KINGDOM

To help us find nourishment in our true King, it's worth looking at the truth of how God establishes His throne, runs His Kingdom, and creates His culture. We want to set our eyes on His throne, not the throne in the oval office, but we can't fully do that if we don't know what the King or His Kingdom are like. In my own life, I've found three questions worth exploring here.

1. What is the throne of God like?

God's throne is described often in the Bible, but a few key verses stand out to me (emphasis added).

> *Righteousness* and *justice* are the foundation of your throne;
> love and faithfulness go before you.
>
> **PSALM 89:14, NIV**

> Let us then with confidence draw near to the throne
> of *grace*, that we may receive mercy and find grace to
> help in time of need.
>
> **HEBREWS 4:16**

> Then the angel showed me the river of the water of life,
> bright as crystal, flowing from the throne of God and of
> the Lamb through the middle of the street of the city;
> also, on either side of the river, the tree of life with its
> twelve kinds of fruit, yielding its fruit each month. The
> leaves of the tree were for the *healing* of the nations.
>
> **REVELATION 22:1-2**

There are some key words to notice here: *righteousness*, *justice*, *grace*, and *healing*. These are attributes of the character of God Himself. God is righteous, restoring what is broken. God is just, righting what is wrong. God is gracious, giving undeserved gifts and favor. God is healing, regenerating the nations. His throne is shaped by His character, and it is His throne that holds all things together (including our political parties) in this beautiful, unexplainable way. This is why God's throne is the highest, why His is the Supreme Court. All other thrones and courts fall short.

2. What is the culture of God's Kingdom?

Jesus lays out the culture of His Kingdom beautifully in His Sermon on the Mount. There in Matthew 5–7, we find what is likely the most well-known description of the Kingdom of God and how we ought to treat one another. But I want to look just a few chapters beyond that. In Matthew 16, Jesus tells us what the culture—the spirit—of His Kingdom is made up of: "If anyone would come after me, let him deny himself and take up his cross and follow me" (verse 16:24).

The culture of this Kingdom? It's about denying ourselves, taking up our cross, and following Him. The culture of the Kingdom of God is full of crosses, not swords, which is the most counterintuitive value to our worldly culture. Our culture says to protect ourselves at all costs, but Jesus says to deny ourselves. Our culture praises grabbing our swords to defend our positions, but Jesus says to put down our sword and take up our cross. Our culture wants us to follow the leader with the most power, but Jesus says we simply need to follow Him.

The moment we start to buy into swords over crosses is the moment we've lost sight of the true Kingdom's culture. This is a struggle of flesh and spirit in our souls. There are so many days in my life where I want to give in to the culture of my flesh. When I don't want to make one more breakfast, serve one more child, fold one more load of laundry, help with one more math problem, tie one more shoe, take one more meal to a family in need, help one more coworker with one more task, admit I was wrong to my husband one more time. I don't want to deny myself. I don't want to serve others. I don't want to put my own agenda down for anyone.

But it's in these unseen places, in these mundane daily rhythms, in these earthly real-life choices that I can start letting the spirit of God win. Then, I can choose to feed my soul by embracing His culture for my home, my family, and myself. I can choose life through death. I can choose to crucify my flesh and let the Spirit lead. I can choose the cross over the sword. I can choose to crown Jesus as King.

And every single time I let His culture permeate my own, my soul is fed. Every single time I give my time away, lay down my agenda, or put away my sword, I find my soul is more alive. I am lighter. I am free. I am nourished.

3. Where is God's Kingdom?

This one may actually be the easiest answer to find! Because God's Kingdom is wherever God is King. This means God's Kingdom can be in your kitchen. And it can also be all the way across the globe in your Nigerian sister's kitchen. Wherever God is worshiped as the rightful King, His Kingdom is being built there. God's Kingdom can flourish right there in your own little plot of earth as you worship God in a myriad of ways. God's Kingdom can grow in your dorm room as you love those who live in your residence hall. It can expand in your living room as you build puzzles with your preschooler and change your baby's diaper with love. It can flourish in your office with a lay-down-your-life attitude toward your coworkers, at the grocery store with a kind word to the cashier, in your neighborhood as you serve the new family next door with fresh cookies. God's Kingdom is built inside of you every time you feed your soul with the truth of His Word and denounce any other kingdom or king threatening to take His place. It grows when you lay down your life for another, when you put away your sword and pick up your cross, when you listen for God's voice and have an adventure of faith.

SUBMISSION

So how do we practice picking up our cross and laying down our sword? How do we practice crowning the one true King and dethroning one political party or president as our savior? The spiritual practice of submission can be a great help to our hearts here.

When we call Jesus our King, we're submitting to His authority, rule, and reign. Untainted, the true definition of submission is to voluntarily come underneath the authority of another. In God's Kingdom, to submit is to make the choice to come underneath the protection and provision of His leadership. But I know that for so many of us, that word has been tainted and abused in the history of the church. Many of us have a bad taste in our mouth when it comes to the idea of submission, so we may need to do some heavy lifting to recover its original meaning. If the idea of submission is a tender spot for you, I am sorry for the experiences that may have led you to this place. May you know God is trustworthy, ready to shelter you, to be a refuge, to be a provider, and to be a protector. He has your good and His glory in mind, which is the best possible scenario.

Think of an umbrella. When it's pouring rain outside and you need to get from here to there, an umbrella protects you. It keeps you from being soaked and provides shelter from the storm. But in order for that to happen, you have to choose to come underneath the umbrella. To submit to someone says you trust them to be your umbrella in the storm. To submit to the Lord means we're choosing to come under His protection and receive His provision. Submission is a daily practice of coming under the good and compassionate umbrella of Christ.

> Submission is a daily practice of coming under the good and compassionate umbrella of Christ.

And as we undertake this practice, may our souls find freedom from fear. May we worship the Supreme King of the Supreme Court. May we live by the righteousness of Christ, the justice of God, the grace given from the Spirit, and the healing that comes from the tree of life. May we find our thirst quenched and our hunger satiated when we lay down our sword and pick up our cross.

A Practice

Take the next week and practice coming underneath the rule and reign of Jesus as King. Consider starting your day by bowing your head or praying on your knees for a few minutes in a posture of humility. Gently explore where you want to rebel, where you want to overthrow Him, and where you've crowned yourself or others as King. Confess this to God openly and honestly and ask Him to help you shift your eyes to His Kingdom and His place as the rightful King in your life.

A Prayer

Take the time to very slowly and deliberately pray through the Lord's Prayer, thinking about God's Kingdom as you do:

> *Our Father in heaven,*
> *hallowed be your name.*
> *Your kingdom come,*
> *your will be done,*
> *on earth as it is in heaven.*
> *Give us this day our daily bread,*
> *and forgive us our debts,*
> *as we also have forgiven our debtors.*
> *And lead us not into temptation,*
> *but deliver us from evil.*
> **MATTHEW 6:9-13**

5

IMAGO DEI

Starved for Justice

It was May 25, 2020.

I was aimlessly scrolling on Instagram that afternoon when my thumb stopped on a conversation two female authors were having about a woman named Amy Cooper. Earlier that morning in Central Park, Cooper, a white woman, called the police on a Black man named Christian Cooper (no relation) who was bird-watching. The two were in an area of the park where dogs were required to be on leash, so Christian asked Amy to leash her dog. At this, Amy retaliated:

> Before calling the cops, she told him that, "I'm gonna tell them there's an African-American man threatening my life," suggesting that she was intentionally

weaponizing a system of police brutality against Black Americans to scare a man who called her out for breaking a minor rule.[1]

Later that same day, Derek Chauvin, a white Minneapolis police officer, killed George Floyd, a Black man, during an arrest after a store clerk wondered if Floyd's twenty-dollar bill was counterfeit. Chauvin pressed his knee on Floyd's neck for nine minutes and twenty-nine seconds while Floyd was hand-cuffed facedown in the street.[2] During the final two minutes, Floyd became motionless and had no pulse, but Chauvin did not relent. He kept his knee on Floyd's neck and back even as emergency medical technicians arrived to treat Floyd.[3] By the time the incident ended, George Floyd was dead.

One day, two videos, four hundred years of racism right in front of my face. Thousands of years of denying the dignity of human life—of oppressing the very image of God inside of Black men and women—played out shockingly in front of my eyes that day.

George Floyd's inability to breathe broke something inside of me. It did the same for so many others for so many reasons. His death unearthed a fight for life. A fight for flourishing. A fight for every person—every image bearer of the Most High God—to live and work and love and drive and walk and shop and even bird-watch in freedom.

Yes, I had long recognized that racism was a cruel reality in our country. I had known that my friends of color weren't always treated the same as I, a white woman, was treated. I knew there was still work to be done. But that day, I realized with sobering pain that there was so much I needed to know. So much I needed to learn. So much I needed to repent of. So much I needed to do.

I love Ibram Kendi's analogy here, as captured in an interview with Brené Brown:

> In America, says Kendi, it's as though racist ideas are constantly rained on your head . . . "You don't even know that you're wet with those racist ideas," because *the ideas themselves lead you to believe that you're dry.* "Then someone comes along and says, 'You know what, you're wet, and these ideas are still raining on your head. Here's an umbrella.'"[4]

Friend, this was my umbrella.

Over the next several weeks, stories tumbled out from my friends of color. Like whispers in the dark, they were stories told through tears. They were stories of microaggressions and daily fears of doing simple things like shopping or driving. Stories of needing to put the wallet—first thing—into the cupholder when they get in the car so police officers won't think they're reaching for a weapon. Stories of heartache, abuse, racism, and discrimination. Stories of not having the freedom to run, to bike, to laugh, to play, to dance. Stories of the fear of not making it home.

My own questions kept me up at night too.

What if George Floyd had been my own brother?

Why does this keep happening?

What is wrong with us? With me?

Where is racism hiding in the spaces, places, and systems that I have around me?

Why do I feel so blinded?

Where am I contributing to a system that benefits me and my white privilege?

Why don't I know about Black culture, Black doctors, Black entrepreneurs, Black Wall Street, Black amazingness? Why do I know so few of their stories?

I wasn't alone in my stark wake-up call. It seemed the whole world rose up for justice, for equity, for dignity, for humanity, for targeted Black folks, for human flourishing. The call to reckon with centuries of racism, of police brutality, of white privilege was loud and clear.

But the thirst for justice is not anything close to new. The parched lips of approximately 472,000 African men, women, and children, branded like cattle and chained together on ships for the Middle Passage, cried out for freedom under the decks of slave ships. The suffocating faces of men and women made in the image of God cried out for centuries, between 1619 and 1860, as they were kidnapped, sold, traded, and dehumanized.[5] And as the false belief that "nonwhite people are less human than white people" continued,[6] so did the iterations of oppression. From reconstruction to racial terror lynching to segregation to presumption of guilt to gerrymandering to gentrification to redlining to racial profiling to criminalization, it continues.

Yes, we are starving for justice.

In the Sermon on the Mount, Jesus speaks to our hunger and thirst, to our starving. He promises that those who hunger and thirst for justice will be satisfied and filled (see Matthew 5:6, NLT). They will be nourished and blessed. He sees the injustice, has compassion upon the oppressed, and will satisfy the hunger for justice. We also know that the Beatitudes weren't prescriptive ("You should be like this so God will love you"). They were descriptive ("Even folks who have experienced such terrible injustice—who hunger for justice—will be filled").

JUSTICE AND RIGHTEOUSNESS

When we think of justice, so many of us think about heeding the law correctly. We think about the laws put in place and the consequences that come when we don't follow them (like the ticket I just received for speeding the other day, with my fourteen-year-old son in the car). In terms of justice, it's a job we assign to the government, to law enforcement, to the people in charge. Many of us lean away from the work of justice, taking a backseat and leaving the bulk of the work to others because we feel underqualified, uncomfortable, or maybe even apathetic.

But friend, this is an approach born out of our own starvation. When we walk away from the work of justice, we have forgotten. We have forgotten Who justice belongs to and what our part is in it. Justice is so much bigger and more beautiful than mere government or a court system! Justice is God's idea. He is just, and He loves justice (see Isaiah 61:8).

The Hebrew word for justice is *mishpat*. That word occurs more than two hundred times in the Hebrew Old Testament.

Simply put, *mishpat* means "acquitting or punishing every person on the merits of the case, regardless of race or social status." But at its root, *mishpat* means so much "more than just the punishment of wrongdoing. It also means to give people their rights." In fact, only 10 percent of justice mentioned in the Bible is in regards to punishment. The other 90 percent? It's all about the proactive protection.[7]

And here's what else I find so interesting: the word *justice* is often paired with the word righteousness. Dozens of times in the Bible, justice and righteousness are mentioned as if they're sisters in God's kingdom. Psalm 89:14 declares, "Righteousness and justice are the foundation of your throne" (ESV). Righteousness is the "day-to-day living in which a person conducts all relationships in family and society with fairness, generosity, and equity."[8] In short, justice is giving people their rights, and righteousness is living rightly among people. Giving rights and living rightly—this is what God's throne is built upon. And in fact, justice and righteousness are *so* close to one another they are sometimes translated one for the other. This happens specifically in the Sermon on the Mount. The NLT says, "God blesses those

> Justice is giving people their rights, and righteousness is living rightly among people.

who hunger and thirst for justice," while the NIV says, "Blessed are those who hunger and thirst for righteousness" (Matthew 5:6). Together, these are pillars of the Kingdom of God. And for us as believers—as members of the body of Christ—they should be pillars of the way we express our faith in this broken, starving world.

IMAGO DEI

So, what exactly does that mean for us? In a world starving for justice—for racial reconciliation specifically—where do we begin?

I think we have to go back to the beginning.

On page one of the Bible, we see the deep significance of how we as humans were created: "God created mankind in his own image, in the image of God he created them; male and female he created them" (Genesis 1:27, NIV).

We were formed in the image of God. The Latin phrase used for this is *imago Dei*, meaning we reflect the divine nature of God Himself. We are unique and set apart from any other creature. Created with dignity, value, and worth, we are made in God's own majestic likeness. That fact alone gives us significance as human beings. It gives us inerrant value—a gift that reminds us we have significance just as we are made. Our very significance is stamped in our souls. We are imago Dei—the image of God. We ought to honor this in ourselves, and we ought to honor it in one another. Our image-bearing dignity demands the respect, honor, and care of one another.

And it also spurs us to live in the image of our Maker. One of the deepest implications of being made in God's image is that we are made to love. God Himself is love (see 1 John 4:8). That being true, as those made in God's image, we are called to reflect that love to others—to *everyone*—around us. We are called to live as loving protectors of God's image in ourselves and others.

Sounds simple, right? Love yourself and love others. Recognize the image of God in one another. We got this, right?

Well, that's where the lies come in.

So many lies happened in the beautiful Garden. So many questions about our identity surfaced from the Snake. So many doubts came in about our own worth and value as humans. So many lines were drawn with that first bite of fruit. And then, the question suddenly became: Are we really as significant as God says we are?

The Snake told the first couple they would be like God if they ate the fruit. The implication? That they weren't already like God, bearing His image in their souls. The Snake tempted them to deny their significance as image-bearers, and sadly, they bought into the lie he was selling. They trusted the Snake more than they trusted God. And with that first bite, they denied their original design.

The result? Shame, division, loss of dignity.

And friend, isn't the same true for us? When we ignore the imago Dei in ourselves or in others, we're denying God-given dignity. Instead of unity in the beautiful body of Christ, we find pain and shame. Instead of reconciliation, we find division. Instead of embracing diversity, we grasp at uniformity. Instead of nourishment, we find starvation.

This is where I think we have to begin in the work of racial justice: by recognizing the imago Dei in one another. By celebrating it, protecting it, rejoicing in it. By loving each other as God's beloved creations, each one a unique representation of His diverse image.

For some of us, the work may need to stop here for a while. We may need to sit in the conviction that we have failed to recognize, love, and stand up for the imago Dei in one another.

We may need to repent of this reality, asking God to change our hearts, our thoughts, our words, our eyes. If we want to find nourishment in our starvation, through justice, we have to start with shifting our hearts to see the imago Dei—the valuable, beloved, beautiful image of God—in every soul of every color.

MY BROTHER'S KEEPER

But friend, this is only the beginning. If recognizing the image of God in one another is where we start, then where do we go from there?

Not too long after the eating of that fruit in the Garden, Cain killed his brother Abel. It's a brutal story found in the pages of Genesis—a harrowing glimpse of what the Fall brought us. When it was all said and done, Cain asked God this important question: "Am I my brother's keeper?" (Genesis 4:9).

The answer for us today is still a resounding YES. You are your brother's keeper, and he is yours. We belong to each other, friend. And that means we are to keep each other accountable. To speak up when we see our brothers and sisters being wronged. To fight for equality for all the brothers and sisters we are called to keep. To love, defend, and celebrate the unique image of God that is stamped on each one of our souls. As Hebrews 13:1 clearly states: "Keep on loving one another as brothers and sisters" (NIV).

Once we see the image of God in each other, we must keep it—protect and honor it—for one another. This is where the real nourishing work of justice begins.

But of course, this is not how we've done things since the Garden. We've shut our eyes to the image of God in those who don't look like the majority. We've refused to be one another's keepers. Or worse, we've refused to keep an image that doesn't resemble our own. We're starving the image of God in ourselves and in others. We have been since the Garden.

The roots of injustice, racism, and white supremacy run all the way back to the Garden. And we have seen those roots dig deeper with every passing day we've allowed racism, hate, and division to remain among us. Instead of being keepers of the image of God in each other, we've chosen simply to keep each other in categories. Instead of owning the imago Dei, we've owned other human beings.

Some people object, saying, "But I haven't ever owned anyone." While that may be true, as my pastor pointed out, it's interesting that we say *we* when it comes to all the good America has done, but we choose *I* when it comes to anything disgraceful in our country's past. *We* have made amazing technological advances, but *I* did not own enslaved people. Whew.

I have done this very thing. But if we're going to practice being one another's keeper—to bring corporate healing to humanity—we must confess the corporate sins of the past. The prophet Nehemiah owned and confessed the sins of his ancestors and asked God for healing. He identified himself with *we* in the sin of idolatry (even thought he had not participated), and he soon tasted the *we* of healing. May we follow his lead.

Friend, I think we have to be honest with ourselves here. I found myself stopped still at the weight of what I saw unfolding online that day. I was shocked, horrified, saddened, outraged. And I knew I had to do something. But before I could take even a step in the direction of righting the wrongs of racial reconciliation, I had to get honest with myself. I've prayed some, and I've cared some. But maybe that wasn't enough. Maybe that was the minimum—the appetizer on the plate of justice. If I wanted to be nourished—to taste the fullness of God's just work of racial reconciliation in our world—I could no longer be satisfied with the minimum.

THE MODEL OF JESUS

Friend, we could stop here. We could sit in the knowledge that all are made in God's image. We could repent of the ways we have failed to recognize that in one another. We could choose to move forward by doing what's in our path to treat other people like they're our brothers and sisters in Christ. But while all of that is good, amazing, life-changing work, it's really just our starting point. If we want to be fully satisfied and fed in the work of justice in this world, we have to go above and beyond that. We have to be willing to do more—the hard, difficult, challenging, Kingdom-living stuff—that stands up and speaks up for the image of God in others.

Thank God for Jesus.

Because we can't possibly do this in our own strength.

We need Jesus.

Because we don't know how to do this.

We need Jesus.

Because we will fumble and fail at this sometimes.

We need Jesus.

Because this isn't going to be easy.

We need Jesus.

Jesus came and showed us what a true image-bearer ought to be. One who heals and helps, who serves and saves, who restores and redeems. He showed us what it is to love God, ourselves, others, and creation. In His life and ministry, we get the model for what real, maximum-level justice work is. Jesus cared for those who were oppressed. He sought out and stood up for the marginalized. He defended those who had been cast out or left behind. He lived His life so that everyone—*all* people of *all* races and *all* ethnicities—would know they were made and loved by God just as they are. And friend, I believe that's the model we're called to follow in this work.

In John 15, Jesus is speaking to His followers about what it looks like to love others as God loves us. And in His words, I find both a challenge and an encouragement to know where to begin: "This is my commandment, that you love one another as I have loved you. Greater love has no one than this, that someone lay down his life for his friends" (John 15:12-13).

If we want to do the Kingdom work of loving and keeping our brothers and sisters, this is where we start. We love as God loved us. We follow the model of Jesus' love for us. It's unconditional, never-ending, always defending. It's strong, lasting, and ours for the taking. It requires nothing of us but to show up and receive it. That's the love we are to give to others.

And how do we show that love to others? To our marginalized, oppressed, overlooked brothers and sisters of other races and ethnicities? By following Jesus' command in the second part of that passage. If we want to love others as Jesus loved us—if we want to live in the great love that Jesus modeled for us—we have to be willing to lay some things down.

As a white woman, this means laying down my discomfort at hearing the stories my friends of color share about their real and harrowing experiences as minorities in this country. It's laying down the arguments that want to bubble out of me when I'm confronted with my own prejudice or bias. It's laying down the desire to turn away from or ignore parts of our history that are hard to reckon with. It's laying down the privileges afforded to me for the sake of those who aren't given the same.

If we want to do the real work here—to not just see and acknowledge the image of God in others but to be willing to defend and honor it no matter what—then we've got to start laying down the stuff that may be standing in our way. We can't fill our hands with the work of justice if we're holding on to these things instead. So friend, we've got to lay them down.

The good news with Jesus is that we aren't in this alone. We have the Spirit of God to help regenerate our hearts, lay down what's holding us back, and lead us to transforming every space we inhabit with real justice. In our homes, workplaces, politics, education, medicine, and every possible sector of culture—we are called to be the ones who bring the truth and love of Christ. Where there is a lack of loving our neighbor, we are called to bring love. Where there is a lack of mercy, we are called to bring mercy. Wherever there is a lack of justice, we are called to bring justice. Where there is a lack of flourishing, we are called to bring flourishing. Where there is a lack of opportunity, we are called to bring opportunity.

Wherever we can, at whatever the cost, we must lay down our defenses for our brothers and sisters.

We must model the love of Jesus, because the love of Christ compels us (see 2 Corinthians 5:14).

TRUTH AND LOVE

I need to tell you that this journey of acting justly has taken and will continue to take some serious soul searching. But, notice, dear one, I didn't say *shame* searching. This is not about shame; nothing grows in shame. Everything grows in love. And truth is an integral part of love.

I began to take a loving look at the truth in my very own life.

Where have I benefited from racial injustice?

What has been my wealth story?

What does it look like to embrace the process of unlearning and relearning, and to not see this as something that I must be perfect at doing?

What would it look like to embrace the long, messy process instead of wishing for some kind of buttoned-up perfection?

I grew up in a 960-square-foot house in West Toledo, Ohio. My parents enrolled us in a Catholic school and highly valued education. My father worked for forty years in the warehouse at Ace Hardware, and my mom worked at the local Jo-Ann Fabrics store part time. They came from humble backgrounds and worked hard. My father put himself through college at the University of Toledo, and my mom graduated high school and started a well-paying job for

Bell Telephone. Before my third-grade year, my parents were able to build a new house in Sylvania, a suburb of Toledo. We doubled our square footage and moved into an award-winning school district, highly ranked in Northwest Ohio for college prep. Good neighborhoods with good schools create good opportunities.

But what was good for me came at the cost of the goodness of others. I was the beneficiary of redlining. Redlining blocked Black families from obtaining home loans and was a major factor in the substantial wealth gap between Black and white families. As property value increases, so does personal wealth. This has played out in a variety of ways.[9]

When the pandemic hit, my mother-in-law (who is white) sent her children money to try to ease any financial burdens we might run into. She has been a homeowner for about fifty years, and has seen her home value increase significantly due to her neighborhood location. But a friend of mine, a Black first-generation college student from Detroit who has experienced the effects of redlining in his community, didn't receive money from his family when the pandemic hit. In fact, he sent any extra he had home to his mom and his brothers.

Many households in Black communities were hit hard by the pandemic and didn't have extra from checking, savings, or generational wealth to lean into. They couldn't afford reliable internet or electronic devices to facilitate remote learning, which put their children at an even greater disadvantage. The pandemic laid bare what has been built into the foundation of our country: a disproportionate privilege for people with white skin.[10]

From generational wealth to my freedom from fearing for my life when pulled over by the police (or even receiving a ticket as a privileged white woman), I have benefited from racial injustice. I have to acknowledge this with truth and love in order to move forward in the work that God has called us to in regards to justice.

In truth and love, I have to ask myself some hard questions.

Where have I ingested white supremacy without even knowing it?

Where am I spending my money?

What businesses am I upholding and why?

What land am I standing on, and have I acknowledged the First Nations of this land?

Where have I diminished the dignity of others—where have I oppressed the imago Dei in others?

I had never even considered some of these challenging questions until I started to see, listen to, and acknowledge the losses my Black and brown brothers and sisters—fellow image bearers—have endured. My dear friend Martha, a brown-skinned Tamilian Indian who is a mother to Blindian boys (Black and Indian) has mentored me in this journey. We have gone on countless walks during which she asked hard questions, brought up thoughts I had never considered, and gently challenged me to see a different story line—all with empathy and grace. As one of the administrators for the Be the Bridge Facebook community, she has highlighted not only the fact that we have stolen people but also that we stole land to start this country.

So I want to acknowledge that I am writing to you from the stolen ancestral lands of Miami and Ozawa and possibly

Shawnee, Wyandotte, Delaware, Iroquois, Kickapoo, Peoria, and Kaskaskia. Our country continues to dehumanize and erase the very people who lived here first. Today, "Native Americans are more likely to be killed by police than people of any other race. Native women are 2.5 times more likely to be raped or sexually assaulted than any other ethnic group, and 97 percent have experienced violence perpetrated by at least one non-Native person."[11] In fact, there is a movement dedicated to missing and murdered indigenous women (MMIW) to end violence against native women. The rise of movements and organizations to protect image-bearing women only shows how profoundly starved for justice we are as human beings. We are starved to experience justice as well as to participate in justice work.

There is a lot of hard truth here, and it is truth I lament. But if we don't acknowledge the truth, how can we heal from it? How can we bring justice to it? How can we celebrate the imago Dei of every tongue, tribe, and nation if we cover up the truth?

Dearly beloved, in Christ we are flawed *and* fully accepted. We are flawed *and* fully loved. We are flawed *and* fully belong to the Father. And in the space of God's great love, we can acknowledge the truth of where we've contributed to the problem—our own biases, prejudices, silences, and more. Because, as Bernice

> We are flawed *and* fully loved. We are flawed *and* fully belong to the Father.

King, Dr. Martin Luther King's youngest child, puts it: "Love is not a weak, spineless emotion; it is a powerful, moral force on the side of justice."[12]

BEGINNING THE WORK IN MYSELF

One of the greatest gifts to me that came from this journey toward justice was the book *Be the Bridge* by Latasha Morrison. As a leader in the work of racial reconciliation and justice in our culture and a brilliant author, leader, and believer in Jesus, Latasha has made it her life's work to bridge communities through her organization Be the Bridge. From her work, I learned a four-step process that I as a white woman could use to do the work in myself before stepping out to do the work in this broken, hurting world.

Friend, this isn't just a box we can check. It's a lifelong practice. But it's one that I believe is not just valuable, but necessary to preserve the Kingdom of God and protect the image of God in one another. As Morrison puts it: "In the love of the family of God, we must become color brave, color caring, color honoring, and not color blind. We have to recognize the image of God in one another. We have to love despite, and even because of, our differences."[13]

I began to walk through Morrison's four steps—the continual process of listening, learning, lamenting, and leveraging—from her book *Be the Bridge*. We can all learn from Morrison, as she has done a brilliant job laying out the path. In reading about her journey and then beginning my own, the process has been incredibly hard but deeply rewarding. It's pulled me out of starvation and toward the nourishment God offers in His image and love. It's helped me find a voice to pull others toward that same healing work.

I believe it could do the same for you.

Listen

Morrison starts with listening because it puts us in a position of humility. Of humbly hearing the real stories of our Black brothers and sisters. As Morrison says: "If you're White, if you come from the majority culture, you'll need to bend low in a posture of humility. You may need to talk less and listen more, opening your heart to the voices of your non-White brothers and sisters."[14] When we bravely ask a friend of color what living in America is like for them, we put ourselves in a place of real connection and empathy. We are saying we are willing to slip on their shoes and walk in them. We make space for others to be heard and held. And if we don't have friends of color? Then we can begin reading stories of Black and brown men and women. We can find resources to help us listen. But remember, the key to listening is to have an ear to hear. To close our mouths and let others have the floor. To honor the imago Dei in front of us.

When I listen to my Black and brown friends talk about their fears and experiences with police officers, I see how I had the privilege of growing up with a positive relationship with police. But when a white male police officer knocked on my brown friend's door in the middle of the day, looking for her son, she was afraid. The officer said he had received a report of "suspicious activity" in another neighborhood across town, with a description of someone who looked like one of her sons. But this was impossible. Her son was several years younger than the individual in question and had been quarantined at home for days. The only connection between the suspect and her son was that the suspect was being chaperoned in a car that looked like hers—a Lexus. My friend was taken aback at having an officer at her door based on a hunch, just because her son happened to be Black. (As it turned out, no crime had been committed—the young man was just going door to door surveying folks.) As a fellow momma myself, my heart broke. When we listen, our eyes open, our soul shifts, our heart breaks.

Learn

Next, Morrison calls us to learn. She says: "You'll need to examine your own life and the lives of your ancestors so you can see whether you've participated in, perpetuated, or benefited from systems of racism."[15] What are you reading, listening to, and researching when it comes to your own racial illiteracy?

One of the smallest but most impactful changes I made was to follow many more people of color on social media. Some are activists, some are racial justice educators, some are actors and actresses. My eyes began to see so many more faces of color, and it was helpful for me to have their images in front of me. What would it look like to make a plan to educate yourself and your kids? There are so many resources celebrating Black doctors, lawyers, musicians, artists, pioneers. It's our job to find them, follow them, and learn from them as we do.

Lament

This one may be the hardest one of all three, because we don't like discomfort. We don't often want to sit in the sadness; we want to fix it. But once we listen to and learn about the tragedies and injustices of our friends and whole communities, we must acknowledge the truth and the pain. This is where we can weep with those who weep. We can grieve because we keep one another close. Morrison teaches: "To lament means to express sorrow or regret. . . . Lament seeks God as comforter, healer, restorer, and redeemer. Somehow the act of lament reconnects us with God and leads us to hope and redemption."[16] Each time I listen and learn something hard, I try to stop and sit with it. Let it sink in. Acknowledge and lament. This is an act of worship, of compassionate attention to the imago Dei in others.

I remember the freedom and ease my husband and I enjoyed as we biked downtown on a date one summer night. We ended up biking back home in the dark, feeling like two giddy high school kids who were out past curfew. And when we talked about our date night with one of our Black friends, he quietly said, "Man. Never. Me and my friends would never bike past dark in this town. We don't feel free to do that. We want to make it home." Initially his confession made me uncomfortable. But over the next few days, I sat with his fear. I closed my eyes and let myself feel the weight of his experience and life in our city. When I wanted to move on, I leaned in to lament. Lament is the beginning of compassion. And compassion fuels justice.

Leverage

Finally, Morrison calls us to leverage what is ours for the sake of others. She says: "We all have some element of privilege in our lives, whether that's the color of our skin, financial status, number of followers on Instagram, or something else entirely. It's what we do with that privilege that can define this work of racial reconciliation in our lives and communities."[17] So the questions are: Where am I leveraging my privilege for my neighbor? What time, resources, abilities, skills can I use to help support, celebrate, and speak up for the image of God in my brothers and sisters of color? How does being an able-bodied white female bring me access to privilege, and how can I leverage that privilege for the sake of those who don't have it? What does it look like to see and serve your neighbor, bringing proactive care and justice to them?

We had finally had a free Saturday. No activities for the kids. No travel. Absolutely nothing. And I wanted to keep it that way. So when my husband sat next to me, hot coffee in hand, and suggested we serve at the downtown food pantry that day? I didn't want to. I wanted to stay in my cozy pj's, in my cozy house, with my cozy resources. All I wanted was comfort. But don't you know God's gentle whisper in my heart became too loud to ignore: "Live this out. Leverage your time for my Kingdom." SIGH. So we did. And that day was such a gift as we built more relationships, as we laughed and shared the load of restocking the pantry, as we gave away our time, our strength, our energy. And we were far from depleted afterwards. God restocked our very souls in the middle of that pantry. We left with faith, hope, and love in our hearts.

My husband and I have shifted from looking only to our own network of friends and family to also seeking out talents and gifts in the community of color. We have chosen to pay

BIPOC for services that we would have previously relied on our white network for, and we look for ways to fund Black initiatives in our city.

Friend, I know this may feel daunting. To me, it certainly did that summer day in 2020. But I must remember how much more daunting it has been and continues to be for those brothers and sisters of color in our country and beyond. If they're tired, weary, afraid, overwhelmed, angry, shouldn't we be with them in their pain? Shouldn't we come alongside the image of God in them? Shouldn't we keep them as our brothers and sisters in Christ?

Perhaps part of finding nourishment is not forgetting where our starvation started. In the Garden. We were in desperate need of justice—of proactive care—after the Fall. And God, in His compassionate grace, gave us justice.

Now friend, it's up to us to walk in that way for the sake of those who bear His image.

For the sake of our brothers and sisters.

A Practice

> Repairing what's broken is a distinctly biblical concept, which is why as people of faith we should be leading the way into redemption, restoration, and reconciliation.
> **LATASHA MORRISON**[18]

Jesus came to bring life and to the fullest. To you, to me, to our communities, to the world. And He is inviting us to join Him in building His Kingdom of life. So where can you begin? Consider the four steps Morrison lays out: listen, learn, lament, and leverage. Which one feels most challenging to you? Where do you need to begin? If you've never taken a step into God's work of justice in our world, start at the beginning. Ask God for ears to hear the stories and experiences of others. Listen first!

A Prayer

As you breathe, let this prayer flow from you.

Inhale: God, I lament my complacency or contributions to injustice.

Exhale: I will walk forward in love, preserving and protecting the image of God in my brothers and sisters.

Going Deeper

If you would like to take the next step but aren't sure where to begin, see the appendix "Action Steps toward Justice."

6

REST IS ON THE WAY

Starved for Sabbath

I find it fitting and even beautiful to end a chapter by encouraging action and movement and begin the next one by encouraging rest and refreshment. Because if we want to be nourished, we need a rhythm that includes both.

I'd like to tell you I have this one figured out and I am the expert to guide you into soul rest and Sabbath practice. Truth be told, this one isn't easy for me. I am naturally prone to striving and averse to resting. As with any and all of these practices, I am fumbling forward. I am a fellow pilgrim. I am a recovering approval addict. I am a busy bee by nature. I am a people pleaser who is continually unraveling the message that my worth is enmeshed in my performance.

I was born with a playful, creative, adventurous, ADHD nature. (My family affectionately called me a space cadet in the eighties, though I am now second-guessing the affection in this.) I had ideas, and I made art, and I wrote in my journal all the time, and my room was a disaster. I was a tornado of creativity and achievement.

Naturally, I started a soap-carving business when I was in the third grade. My amazing dad invested in this "business" and bought my best friend and me a twenty-four pack of Ivory bar soap to carve. We carved one bar that looked like a mangled sea turtle. Bless his heart. Bless ours. Needless to say, the rest of the soap was inconspicuously shoved under our beds for two solid years.

After our soap-carving aspirations collapsed, I dreamed of hosting my own talk show like Oprah. I saw it as an avenue for doing two things I loved: entertaining others and doing very important, world-changing work. Even though my heart was in the right place, I found myself dreaming these dreams for one reason: to be loved. I was entertaining to be loved. I was performing to be loved. I was trying to prove that I was capable and in turn, lovable.

I didn't know this at the time, of course. I couldn't have told you that was why I was filling my schedule to the brim. I liked being involved in several sports and found a great deal of identity there. I liked holding important positions at school and youth group. I saw leadership qualities emerge and grow in me there. I liked being liked (and don't we all?). I thought I was staying busy and being productive in order to chase my dreams and make an impact. But in reality, I was staying busy and productive so others would know that I was important.

The more responsible we are, the more responsibility we'll receive. If we seem to carry it all so well, then others will pile on more . . . if we let them. After growing up as a childhood achiever, I inadvertently led the world to believe I could take it all on and do it well. That pattern continued into my early adult years, and eventually, I found myself becoming resentful of people's unrealistic expectations of me (as if they were the problem!). Anger simmered below the surface each time people asked more from me. I was trying to keep my appearance well-balanced, keep my family well-ordered, and corral the chaotic house clutter into its place. The salient space I forgot? My own starving soul.

A COVER-UP

Managing other people's expectations and opinions is not only exhausting, it is soul-depleting. When we carry others' opinions, our arms aren't free to do the work we were created to do.

> When we carry others' opinions, our arms aren't free to do the work we were created to do.

When we listen to other people's voices, our souls can't hear our own song. When we fill our calendars with busyness, we leave no room for the deep, peaceful rest our souls really need to survive.

Why do we do that?

Why don't we rest? What keeps us needing to be so busy?

Why do we just keep going and filling up our calendars? Why are we always hurrying and running our kids ragged while we're busy proving we're actually very important? Why is it so hard to trust that resting is good? That it's actually a nourishing act of faith?

Because busy is safe.

Busy is meaningful.

Busy is important.

Busy is an identity.

And busy covers up fear.

Fear can be a scout for us, if we choose to listen to her. Fear helps us ask some pretty good questions, if we can give honest answers. What am I afraid will happen if I just stop? If I create a rhythm that intentionally includes rest? If I take the time in silence to renew my mind? What do I fear if I say no to this next project? What am I scared will happen if I just let go of opinions and expectations? What fears is my busyness trying to cover up?

I'm afraid I won't be worth anything.

I'm afraid I won't be necessary.

I'm afraid if I don't keep everything running smoothly at high speed, then I won't matter.

I'm afraid I have to run the world to be important in it.

I'm afraid I won't be needed by anyone.

I'm afraid I won't like what I find in the quiet.

I'm afraid I won't be loved and admired.

I'm afraid I won't find fulfillment.

I'm afraid I won't know who I am without the busy.

This is a lot to carry—an exhausting load. I'm tired just thinking about it!

I imagine your confessions might sound the same. Because for so many of us, busyness is a cover-up. A cover-up of the fear of exposing who we really are without our schedules, our achievements, our accolades, and our ability to meet everyone's needs and expectations perfectly.

But busy is leaving us more than just tired and afraid. Deep down, it's leaving us hungry. In all that busyness, we don't find satisfaction. Ultimately, we just find starvation. That's because busy certainly isn't a fruit of the Spirit. In fact, keeping in step with the Spirit may not look like busyness at all. As Paul tells us, the result of walking alongside the Spirit of God looks like this: love, joy, peace, patience, kindness, goodness, faithfulness, gentleness, and self-control (see Galatians 5:22-23). I don't know about you, but when I am so busy being busy, my life doesn't look much like any of these things. I mostly just feel afraid.

That's when it's helpful to remember that God has not given us a spirit of fear. So if the only fruit we're producing is stale and afraid, maybe it's time to check which spirit we're walking with: Is it the Spirit who produces life-giving fruit or the spirit whose fruit starves us for more?

A RHYTHM OF REST

When God created everything in the very good beginning, He worked for six days. And in those six days, He literally made everything—light and oceans and creatures and sky and night and humans in His image. Basically, God was busy! But then on the seventh day, something different happened. Then, God rested.

But this wasn't just some measly nap. It wasn't just clearing His schedule to have some time off. It wasn't a veg-out-on-the-couch-and-watch-Netflix kind of thing. This was real, deep, soul-nourishing rest. It was blessed rest. Set apart rest. Holy rest.

There's a rhythm here—a pattern at play that God Himself participated in to show us the way. He made mountains, and brought beauty, and orchestrated oceans for six straight days. He literally did it all! And then, He rested.

Work, then rest.

That's the rhythm God created the world with. It's the pattern He laid out for us to follow in our own spiritual lives.

Work, then rest.

What's crazy to think about here is the fact that God is God. And in that, God doesn't actually *need* rest. God is limitless and all powerful. Nothing is too hard for Him (see Jeremiah 32:17). He does not get tired (see Isaiah 40:28-31). He does not slumber and watches over us when we do (see Psalm 121:3-4). He never runs out of energy, out of sustainability, out of Himself. So, if God doesn't need the rest, why did He take it? He clearly made a deliberate choice to rest—a choice made out of love for us. By setting the Sabbath apart from the beginning, God established a rhythm of work and rest for us to implement in our own lives—a pattern of sweat and trust for us to follow.

We see this rhythm play out again and again and again in God's Word. In fact, it's so valuable to Him that it was built into the Ten Commandments given to Moses. It's the fourth commandment, and it's serious business. And as humans tend to do, if something feels religiously serious, we really make sure we get it right. We make more laws around the law to make sure the law is super lawful.

We all do this. We make these little rules in our hearts to try to ensure that we can check off the God box. We make little spiritual deals in our hearts.

If we shouldn't have sex before we're married, I am not kissing until the altar.

If we don't want our brother to stumble, we are going to only wear one-piece swimsuits and definitely not spaghetti straps.

If we shouldn't get drunk, we will never, ever set foot in a bar. You get the picture.

The Sabbath was soon so bogged down with extra tiny rules on how to keep it set apart, God's people seemed to have forgotten about the heart—the rhythm—behind the command. It wasn't about the thirty-nine "clarifications" added to this command, including no kneading, tying, untying, reaping, plowing, or baking. (Baking is one of my favorite things to do on the Sabbath, by the way.) The heart behind the Sabbath is in the rhythm it gives us for life. It's so much more than a command; it's a gift! The Sabbath is grace to us—one God knew we would need. It's a gift that encourages us to walk in His rhythm and to trust Him to provide when we do.

THE PRACTICE OF REST

When I first started reading about the good gift of the Sabbath, I felt really overwhelmed. A whole entire day of *not* working? Of *not* preparing for the next week? Of *not* getting ahead or catching up? I have so much to do! How could I possibly stop for even a moment, let alone an entire day!

In that season, I found great comfort and encouragement from Marva Dawn and her book *Keeping the Sabbath Wholly*. She writes:

> Setting aside a holy Sabbath means that we can cease our productivity and accomplishments for one day in every seven. The exciting thing about such a practice is that it changes our attitudes for the rest of the week. It frees us up to worry less about how much we produce on the other days . . . .
>
> I desperately need to keep Sabbaths faithfully so that this attitude can increasingly pervade the rest of my days.[1]

Ceasing productivity and accomplishment for an entire day once seemed like only a dream. To be honest, it seemed impossible. Are we really allowed to do that? Dawn says yes. And more importantly, God says yes. So, we can say yes too.

Friend, not only are we allowed to rest, but God encourages us to rest. God encourages us to lay down our efforts and identity tied to productivity every seven days. God encourages us to find nourishment for our tired, starving souls in our rest.

Dawn calls this a "practice," and I think that's right. Over the past fifteen years, the practice of a Sabbath has brought such spiritual nourishment in my life, but I had to give myself room to figure it out. As with any practice, it takes time. We have to train for it. We start small and build up. And of course, we're going to get it wrong a time or two. Every good practice includes both the learning and the failing . . . on repeat!

But the practice is worth it. The practice is what gets us there.

I need to continue to learn that I am not the sum of my accomplishments. I need to remind myself constantly that my worth is not tied to my productivity. I need to make rest a practice in my life to remember what really feeds my soul. I think the same is true for you, friend! After all, we are human beings, not human doings, and that means we are loved and valuable simply by being. When we create space to rest—to simply be—we are creating space to allow God to speak that reminder over us.

Our society is thirsty for the good and holy practice of setting aside our own work and resting in God's acceptance of us through the Cross. That's the *real* rest. That's *soul* rest. There, we can be loved, held, and enjoyed by Jesus. There, we can allow His face to shine upon us. There, we can untangle our identity from our work and place it in being God's. There, we can be nourished.

Recently I found myself so depleted one afternoon in the middle of the week. I was looking at a to-do list a mile long, at the top of which was my sermon for our church service that coming Sunday. It was one of those moments where I needed to just trust God, surrender to the fatigue, and lie down for a few minutes. In the past, I would've done the exact opposite. I would've made every attempt to run through that list with all kinds of busyness and frenzy. I would've written a hurried sermon under the stress of performing, and it likely would've been terrible.

But this was the new me—the me who'd made rest a practice in my life. So instead of going, I stopped. I rested . . . quite literally. When I woke up after a twenty-minute power nap, I had three points in my mind to go with the Scripture I was teaching on that week. Still groggy, I wrote those down and gave myself permission to take my time waking up. Then, the following day, I sat down to write my sermon. And I couldn't believe how easily it seemed to come together. In my rest, God led me. He gave me the outline for exactly what I needed to teach just a few days later.

While I rested, God provided.

And friend, I believe He will do the same for you. He's given us the rhythm of rest to nourish our souls. He's asked us to trust Him to care for us in the being rather than the doing. He's asked us to make rest a practice in our lives. If rest is an act of trust, then let it open our eyes and hearts to trust that God loves to provide for us in our faith!

THE MANNA

So how do we begin this journey? How do we start practicing trusting God to sustain His world and to provide for us? How do we Sabbath?

We remember the manna.

In Exodus 16, God hears the Israelites' grumbling about their hunger in the desert. In response, God promises to rain down bread from heaven for them each morning to provide for their needs. He instructs them to gather up an omer (about three pounds) for each person for the day. No more, no less.

If they tried to save it for later or hoard it for themselves, it would've been maggot infested by the next day. That's some really fresh bread God is providing, huh? So fresh, it's intended to eat within the day.

This manna—the daily bread—was a call to trust God's daily provision. The Israelites needed to trust that each morning, God would provide new, fresh bread. They didn't need to hoard or store up for themselves. They just needed to trust and remember that God had it covered each day.

And here's the kicker! On the Sabbath—their sacred day of rest—God promised to do more. The day before the Sabbath, God promised to provide twice as much so that the Israelites wouldn't need to go out and gather on the actual day of rest. They didn't have to do anything to provide for themselves that day. God gave them more simply so they could rest.

The idea of a Sabbath could have been just as frightening to the Israelites as it can be for us. In our efficiency-obsessed, productivity-driven, and capitalistic culture, it's daunting to think about putting it all down simply to rest. In our world, we simply aren't supposed to be able to handle not doing anything. Though times have changed a lot since the days of wandering in the desert, I imagine the Israelites might've felt the same way. Can you imagine the other cultures around them working hard, farming and gathering food for themselves all the time? Then God tells them to do the opposite? To rest for an entire day each week? To let Him take care of it all? It was essentially asking them to take a major trust fall each and every week.

And honestly, it's the same for us. No, we're not looking for God to drop literal manna from the sky each day to meet our physical needs. But we are looking to Him to provide the spiritual manna—the daily bread we need to satiate our souls. And that isn't easy to do all the time. If you're anything like me, you look for the manna, but you do so with a question in your heart:

If God is truly God, is He big enough to be God when we do nothing to provide for ourselves?

That question is real. And that's hard. If we practice a day of rest, we have to ask that question, and we have to answer it honestly. Then, we can remember the manna. We can practice trusting God. In our rest, we can remember that He is good, He is God, and He will provide.

> In our rest, we can remember that He is good, He is God, and He will provide.

I could give you story after story of how trusting God yielded better fruit than my own toil could've ever produced. There was the time my husband was out of town, but I still chose to Sabbath on my own. I woke up from an afternoon nap (yes, while my kids played Minecraft) to a myriad of texts. I was scheduled to speak at a college ministry's weekly meeting in just two days, and they were asking about my PowerPoint notes. Normal stuff, right? Well, usually I'd say yes, but in this case, not so much. Because somehow, this particular speaking event was not on my calendar. This was all news to me! I had planned on taking the whole day to rest, but those text messages changed the plan. Suddenly, besides single parenting all week, I was now also scrambling to have something to present. I was completely blindsided and immediately overwhelmed.

I sat straight up, scurried to find my computer, and started brainstorming for my talk. And in that moment, I had a face-off with my own heart. *Do I trust God to provide for me in this? Or do I trust myself and get to work? If I keep resting—keep choosing what is good for my soul in this moment—will God actually provide the time, the resources, the energy, and the ideas tomorrow? Shouldn't I use the time I have right now to put this together?*

I looked at the assigned topic one more time. This time, it triggered something: a blog post I had recently written. Wait a minute. Wasn't that title of their series the exact title of my post? Had I written this thing already and didn't know it? Did God provide for me already?

Yes.

I pulled up my blog. This was the exact thing the students were asking to hear about at their meeting. It was all set! I had already written exactly what they needed, and God knew it all along. Psalm 139 rang in my ears: "All the days ordained for me were written in your book before one of them came to be" (verse 16, NIV).

God knew about my struggle to Sabbath and to trust Him before this moment came to be. He provided for me way before I needed it, like the manna for two days for the Israelites. We must remember the manna when we start to replace our busyness with rest. We must remember that God will provide.

PREPARE FOR THE SABBATH

And we must also remember how Jesus handled the Sabbath. True to His character, Jesus did good things on the Sabbath.

There were several healings and miracles that Jesus performed specifically on the Sabbath. Of course, the religious leaders of the day were furious when this happened. Because the Sabbath was buried under rules and more laws, they missed that the Sabbath was about God and His goodness. And according to Jesus, goodness included healing.

On one Sabbath, Jesus was in the synagogue. There He met a man with a withered hand. Looking to bring charges against Jesus, the Pharisees asked Him if it was lawful to heal on the Sabbath.

> He said to them, "If any of you has a sheep and it falls into a pit on the Sabbath, will you not take hold of it and lift it out? How much more valuable is a person than a sheep! Therefore it is lawful to do good on the Sabbath."
> MATTHEW 12:11-12, NIV

Then, Jesus completely restored this man's hand.

The religious leaders were so concerned about what not to be doing on the Sabbath that they missed the good they could be doing. Haven't we been there too? I know I have! I've certainly been so concerned with not doing the wrong thing that I missed the good and right thing. This often happens when I am concentrating on God's rules—believing He's out to smite me—instead of concentrating on God's love for me—believing He's out to provide for me. In the former, I find more starvation, but in the latter, I find satisfaction.

To help me get my mind around what is good and helpful for me to do on the Sabbath, I've learned to actually take the time to prepare for the Sabbath. As we often rest on Sundays, I'll use my Saturdays to get my week in order. To get chores done. To get groceries. To do laundry. But when darkness is near on Saturday night, I try to put all signs of work away. My computer, the broom, my to-do list—it all goes away. It gives me room to remember and rest.

In our family, we've also gone through phases of lighting two candles to start the Sabbath. Traditionally, one candle symbolizes remembering the Sabbath and the other observing (as stated in Exodus 20:8 and Deuteronomy 5:12). This practice is an outward symbol to remind us of the inward nourishment our souls will find in the rhythm of rest God created us for.

So, consider what this might look like for you. What does your Sabbath look like, and how can you start preparing your heart, your mind, your family, your home to find rest? I've heard it said, if you work with your hands during the week, then use your mind during the Sabbath. If you work with your mind, then use your hands. Maybe that framework would be a helpful place for you to start!

Remember, rest looks different for all of us. This could mean any number of things depending on what truly quiets and calms your soul.

Rest from comparison: believe that God delights in you. You don't need to look like anyone else. He made *you* on purpose.

Rest from screens: put away your phone and get outside.

Rest from work: do something you've been wanting to do, just for soul pleasure.

Rest from hustle: refuse to make a to-do list. And take
a nap!

Rest from a scarcity mindset: embrace the abundance
God has given you and be generous to specific people.

Rest from productivity: have people over for a meal and
linger. No agenda required.

Rest from self-focus: look for God. Rest in Him. Look
for His gifts, His beauty, His love for you and others.

Rest from complaining: find a real pen and actual paper
and write ten things you are thankful for.

Rest from self-sufficiency: trust God to double your time
and provide for you while you rest.

But friend, let me urge you here again to resist adding rules
to your rest. We want to take a day to practice remembering
God, our Provider. This is not about getting it right. It is about
knowing and loving God and letting Him nourish our tired
and weary souls. It is about resting in the work Jesus did on
the Cross so we would be accepted by Him. It is about celebrating that no other work, or pushing, or proving makes us
acceptable and loved by Him. It's about doing what's good for
you and for others in that time.

Eugene Peterson tells us, "If we do not regularly quit work
for one day a week we take ourselves far too seriously."[2] I love
the rhythm of work and rest and the ancient Sabbath goodness
we can learn from it. Literally write it into your calendar, and
tell everyone you are booked solid during that time. You are
busy resting. You are busy trusting in the Lord. You are busy
finding nourishment for your soul.

A Practice

Plan to rest. Look at your calendar for the next week and block out a few hours (or a whole day) to Sabbath. What does your heart need in order to Sabbath? Do you need nature? Do you need a nap? Do you need to put away some things? Do you need a babysitter for your kids? Take the time to be intentional about your plan to rest.

A Prayer

Part of Sabbath is trusting God. Trusting that He is good and He will provide for you when you rest. Open your Bible and read the verses below aloud as a prayer, asking God to help you remember who He is.

Nothing is too hard for Him (see Jeremiah 32:17).

He does not get tired (see Isaiah 40:28-31).

He does not slumber (see Psalm 121:3-4).

Close by praying, "God, I am worthy of rest. This is the rhythm You created for me. Help me to remember that when I rest, You will always provide what I need."

7

A PLATE FULL OF ANXIETY

Starved for Peace

I was getting my kids ready for school, attempting to make it out the door on time that busy morning. We were bumping book bags and lunches, tripping over shoes and projects, and generally scrambling to get it together. Outwardly, it was complete and total chaos in our home that day.

And inwardly, my mind was no better. It mirrored the chaos as anxious thoughts tripped over each other one after another.

Dinner will be saltine crackers and a side of six-month-old olives if I don't get to the store.

How do I fix my middle child's fear of not belonging?

There's so much laundry to do and someone may be wearing swimsuit bottoms for underwear tomorrow.

How do I stay on top of my oldest son's recent health flare-up? This work deadline is coming fast.

My husband's business travel is increasing, and I don't know how I can add more to my to-do list.

Anxiety had pulled up a seat at the table of my mind and filled my plate with thoughts that were only meant to starve me.

As I flung open the front door, giving hurried hugs and quick kisses and sending my kids running to the bus, I just barely avoided a twisted ankle trying to sidestep an oddly placed box on my porch. The box interrupted my harried activity. It forced me to redirect in order to take a giant step over it. I had to deal with it.

The brown cardboard box was a sizable square with a card on top. I had no clue what it was or when it had arrived. As the bus pulled away, I took a breath, turned around, and casually grabbed the box, expecting it to be light as a feather as I carried it inside. Unexpectedly, I almost dropped it; it was so much heavier than I thought!

I heaved it onto the dining room table, and my curiosity grew as I opened the card. Our last name was misspelled on the note, and the handwriting wasn't one I recognized. The tall, slanted cursive script simply read: "May blessings of honey flow."

I opened up the box to find twelve jars of gorgeous, amber-colored local honey. This was easily over a hundred dollars' worth of honey! It had been left on my porch as a generous gift—so generous that I immediately teared up.

God had done it again.

Honey is the only sweetener my son can have on his diet. Because of that, we go through it in our home like water. You guys, honey is not cheap like sugar. And local honey with all its allergy blockers? Priceless! Someone out there was clearly enjoying the abundance of God's richness and wanted to pour their abundance on us.

I sensed a profound peace, love, joy: God is taking care of us. He sees us. He is with us. He will provide for us. God's abundance rendered my anxiety speechless. We were on our last jar of honey, and God knew it. And if He knows about our little honey need, He knows about it *all*. He knows about the deadlines, and the fears, and the lists, and the need for belonging, and the overgrown grass, and the wounds of rejection, and the long hours at the office, and the huge rifts in our marriage, and the unexpected car repair, and the fear of failure. He knows the late-night worry about our children's math gaps and the early morning stress of a big presentation. He knows about the fears of singleness, the pain of divorce, the mess of marriage. He knows about it all. He sees it all. And He has gifts for it all. He wants to provide peace in our anxiety, and He wants to do so from His abundance.

If we let it, God's generosity can put a much-needed kink in our anxiety.

GROUNDED IN PEACE

There seems to be a strong connection between our anxiety and a scarcity mindset. A scarcity mindset dwells on what we do not have. Like a slow faucet drip, scarcity says there won't be enough time or resources or ideas or ability or any number of things. Thinking scarcity thoughts brings stress, anxiety, fatigue, hoarding, fear, and isolation. It's restrictive and tiresome. It's a kind of closed-grip living. A starved way of life.

But an abundance mindset? One set on the overflowing goodness and unending generosity of our God? The thinking that trusts that God is indeed a good, good Father who loves to provide for His children? This mindset is full of peace, joy, energy, generosity, curiosity, hope, and community. It is full of freedom, tenderness, and openhanded living. It is full of nourishment for our anxious souls.

So how do we move away from a life of worry toward one of peaceful trust in the abundance of God? How do we keep the promise of front-porch honey at the forefront of our minds? How do we stay at peace in a world full of anxiety which invades our minds with relentless speed? How do we stay anchored in peace with news at our fingertips, compounding worry at a pace generations before us didn't have to process?

We practice grounding—grounding for our bodies, grounding for our minds, grounding for our souls.

GROUNDING FOR OUR BODIES

Let's start with our bodies. In the immensely wise book *Try Softer*, Aundi Kolber writes as a mental health therapist, trauma survivor, and master at providing resources for dealing with pain, anxiety, and trauma. One of the tools she suggests is the practice of grounding.

Grounding is a form of mindfulness that helps us become hyper-present to the immediate moment using our five senses (what can you see, hear, smell, taste, feel?). Practicing grounding can provide a buffer from something that may feel distressing while still tapping into our bodies' natural ability to process pain. Once we can learn foundational skills like grounding, we can build on them at our own pace.[1]

The honey box was an unintentional grounding moment for me. It interrupted my anxiety and provided a buffer from my distress. I saw the box with my eyes, almost tripped over the box with my feet, I carried the box with my arms, I opened the honey jar with my hands, I smelled the sweetness with my nose, I tasted the goodness with my mouth. I became hyper-sensitive to the immediate moment, and that moved me from a disintegrated state to an integrated one. My body (tasting the honey) was connected with my mind (thinking about the gift of honey), and I was integrated. This was quite a contrast to my previous disintegrated state: my body in the kitchen with my kids but my mind all over the city, mentally running errands and frantically solving problems. Fortunately, a grounding moment was hoisted on my front porch that morning like an anchor flung in the sand. It calmed me, it fed me, and it gave me peace.

But that's not always the case, is it? What about when anxiety keeps coming? When nothing plops itself in the way of it to ground us? This is where the hard work comes in. If we imagine anxiety as waves in the ocean, flowing into us over and over, we can also visualize some choices about what we'll do in the face of those waves. We can either yield to the waves, allowing them to toss us around and pull us in over our heads, or we can firmly plant our feet in the shallow waters and ground ourselves in what is true and solid in the moment. Obviously, we want to stand grounded, firm, and unmoving. But often, getting there is not a linear path. It's an ebb and flow, back and forth, tossing and flailing, until we find our footing. Taking a moment to ground our bodies in the face of the waves of anxiety is a great place to start.

When we practice grounding with our bodies, we're using our senses to tell us we are safe. My therapist suggests that when I find anxiety rising and starving me of any kind of peace, I can begin to find calm again by grounding through a simple body scan. Maybe this practice will work for you, too! Start at the top of your head and slowly move down your body in your mind's eye. Relax your eyes, release the tension you may be holding in your neck, slow your breathing. You may even put a hand to your heart to connect to your body. This is not a time to judge your body; it's a time to be compassionate and to acknowledge what she is feeling. To graciously pay attention to the resilient body she is. To stop the starvation and start looking for peace.

As I am typing about this grounding exercise, I feel my bare feet on the wide-plank pine floor in my bedroom. I release the tension in my belly with a fuller, longer exhale. I allow my breath to be slower and steady. I feel the weight of the world leave my shoulders. Then, I choose to trust God with what's coming next in my day.

Grounding work can be done anywhere, at any time, in any moment of anxiety. Breathing—the vital gift of life—is available to us anywhere we are. It's the grounding option we carry with us at all times. When we exhale a bit longer than we inhale, our body is telling our brain that we are safe. Anxiety specialist Sarah Tuckett says that the "long, slow exhale is what calms your nervous system and takes you down into that lovely 'rest and digest' (parasympathetic) state."[2] In other words, just the practice of grounding our bodies in our breath will slow our anxious response and make space for peace to take its place.

GROUNDING FOR OUR MINDS

Along with grounding for the body, we can practice grounding for the mind. And as people of faith, this one is so important! Because for us, grounding our minds begins in the Word. When we incorporate the daily practice of reading and memorizing God's Word into our lives, we're planting an anchor of peace in the middle of an ocean of anxiety.

But again, this is a practice, and practice takes time. While God's peace can quiet our starving in an instant, we can access that peace a little bit easier when we have it already written on our minds. To do that, we're going to have to practice a little mental meal replacement. We have to replace the mindless scroll on our phones first thing in the morning (yes, I do that too!) with a mindful meditation and reading of Scripture. Anchoring our minds in peace first thing in the morning will help us access that peace more easily throughout the day.

I remember the first time I let God's Word really shape my day. I was in my college apartment reading the Psalms. I was lying on top of my hunter green comforter (it was the nineties, people!) on the bottom of the bunk bed I shared with my roommate. I had time in between classes, so with a gentle breeze blowing through my window, I used that time to connect with the Lord. The words about the morning jumped off the page: "Listen to my voice in the morning, LORD. Each morning I bring my requests to you and wait expectantly" (Psalm 5:3, NLT).

The writer was asking to be heard by God. He had multiple requests when it came to his day, so he was bringing them to God first thing in the morning. First things first, right? And then after sitting down with God (which I like to imagine happened over breakfast), the writer waited expectantly throughout the day to see how God would provide for him.

I felt my body sigh with relief. Could I do that too? Could I bring all my requests to God and wait expectantly for Him to answer them each morning? I loved the thought of starting my day with sharing all of my thoughts, fears, hopes, and requests with my Creator. This felt like an adventure to have with God Himself. We could meet up in the morning, I would lay all my requests on the table, and I would walk through my day with expectations in my heart. I imagined He would give a wink and smile, saying, "Do you trust me?" And we would set off together, the expectation of God's provision anchoring me to peace anytime I felt tempted toward anxiety.

But there have been long seasons since when I have gotten away from this practice. My phone became my first grab again each morning. I let the news shape my perspective and my social media feed tell me who I am. And just like that, I was slowly starving as I feasted on everything but God's Word. It's a practice, right? In those seasons, I had to be intentional about practicing grounding my mind and feeding it with truth each day. I had to start over. Thank God for the grace to do just that!

If you are finding anxiety and overwhelm rising in your days, try going to God first. I have a journal to write out my thoughts, fears, hopes, and requests after I read or listen to God's Word. I spend time in God's Word, not only to just read it but to memorize it. Having it in our minds is the best way to let God's Word actually shape how we think throughout the whole day. It's the best way to access the peace that will feed us. If you're looking for a place to begin, let me recommend Psalm 23, a passage I've memorized to anchor me. Because my anxiety is often tied to scarcity, grounding myself in the generosity of God brings peace.

My husband and I recently had a few days away without our children to celebrate twenty years of marriage. We were carefree, phone free, and worry free. But as soon as the plane took flight to bring us back home, back to work, back to our responsibilities, I felt anxiety rise. Thankfully, I was holding the book *Life without Lack* by Dallas Willard. His thesis is that Psalm 23 is a way of life—a way to live in the fullness of God without fear or anxiety. As the plane ascended through the clouds, I reflected on the truth of that Psalm.

God will supply all of my needs.
I have more than enough.
God goes with me wherever I go.

God is a God of abundance.

My body, mind, and soul eased as I thought about God's abundance, generosity, and love.

There will be time.

There will be resources.

There will be hope.

There will be restoration.

There will be love.

There will be friendship.

There will be grace.

There will be peace.

My cup overflows because God overflows it. It's not just filled up to the top; I have enough and more—so much so that it is spilling over onto the table. All of that comes with the peace of God in our minds. Knowing God's Word, memorizing it, singing it, orally passing it on to others—it's an act that feeds our starving minds the peace they desperately need.

GROUNDING FOR OUR SOULS

One of the best ways I have learned to ground my soul through anxiety is to go ahead and sink the ship. This is what I mean: picture the very bottom—the very worst-case scenario. See if God will be at the very bottom of the ocean, the very worst, the very darkest place you fear. The house burns down, you lose your job, your loved one dies, your child walks away from Jesus, you are cheated on, you suffer immense pain. What will happen if the ship sinks? If one of your worst fears comes true? Think about that scenario playing out, but include God in the picture. Because, friend, there's only one thing that can possibly break our fall when all else is broken and falling. We will find that God's love will hold. God's love will be at the bottom. God's love *is* the actual bottom.

We know this is true because nothing can separate us from His expansive, deep, unfathomable, rich compassion. No worst-case scenario will be void of Him standing next to us in it.

> I'm absolutely convinced that nothing—nothing living or dead, angelic or demonic, today or tomorrow, high or low, thinkable or unthinkable—absolutely *nothing* can get between us and God's love because of the way that Jesus our Master has embraced us.
>
> ROMANS 8:38-39, MSG

God will be at the bottom of the worst-case scenario. In fact, God is at the top of His game when all is lost. He has been known to take the most terrible thing we imagine and make it beautiful. He has turned crucifixion to celebration, graves to gardens, death to life. He is the God who pulls the best out of the worst, every single time.

> **God will be at the bottom of the worst-case scenario. In fact, God is at the top of His game when all is lost.**

JESUS IS OUR GUIDE

We see Jesus go to the very bottom the night before He was betrayed, abandoned, rejected, beaten, humiliated, and crucified.

This was the absolute worst-case scenario. As Jesus considered the cup before Him—one that overflowed with pain, trauma, and torture—He went to the ground. As a tidal wave of anxiety came over Him, He went down. His grounding came from knees bent, mind centered on the Father, soul ministered to by angels.

> He withdrew about a stone's throw beyond them, knelt down and prayed, "Father, if you are willing, take this cup from me; yet not my will, but yours be done." An angel from heaven appeared to him and strengthened him. And being in anguish, he prayed more earnestly, and his sweat was like drops of blood falling to the ground.
>
> LUKE 22:41-44, NIV

Jesus' response is our guide in our worst-case scenarios. He drops to His knees, His body feeling the external earth in the middle of His internal earthquake. He prays with His mind, asking for what He needs from His good Father. He connects His soul to the spiritual realm as an angel incredibly comes to be by His side and strengthen Him. I have to imagine that this verse from Psalm 23 might have been playing in His mind:

> Even though I walk through the valley of the shadow of
> death,
> I will fear no evil,
> for you are with me;
> your rod and your staff,
> they comfort me.
>
> PSALM 23:4

A rod was for protection, and a staff was for correction. To fend off enemies and to bring sheep back onto the safe path. In this moment, Jesus needed both.

Appallingly, the cup did not pass Jesus. He drank the bitter poison of our sin and suffering. He went to hell and back, walking through the worst possible scenario. And three days later, He could claim the end of that same passage in Psalm 23 as true:

> You prepare a table before me
>> in the presence of my enemies;
> you anoint my head with oil;
>> my cup overflows.
> Surely goodness and mercy shall follow me
>> all the days of my life,
> and I shall dwell in the house of the LORD
>> forever.

PSALM 23:5-6

The morning of His resurrection, the gravesite became a glorious garden. He was the Anointed One, the Messiah, the Victorious One. Jesus drank the cup of death so our cup of life could overflow. And now and forevermore, Jesus will dwell in the house of the Lord.

We can find satisfaction in God's peace, even in our darkest places.

In His own response to the worst moment in His life, Jesus guides us to follow His lead. He teaches us to place our certainty in God in the most uncertain of valleys. Rather than stay starved in our anxiety, we can find satisfaction in God's peace, even in our darkest places. We can bank on what Psalm 23 teaches: "Even though I walk through the valley of the shadow of death, I will fear no evil, for you are with me" (Psalm 23:4).

Why can we fear no evil? Because God Himself is with us. Which is perhaps why the blood-sweat dripped down Jesus' face. He was about to be abandoned by His Father, so we would never be abandoned. He faced the lack of God's presence, so we would never lack. He went through death's valley without God, so we would never face another valley without Him.

As we face anxiety, may we stay grounded in who we are and Whose we are. May we feed ourselves with the peace of God. May we practice standing firm in our belovedness as the waves of anxiety crash and the water of fear rolls down our faces. And there, may we find peace in the presence of God.

A Practice

The daily reading of God's Word helps us hold on to peace when anxiety threatens to starve us. So, consider how you can make that a daily practice in your life this week. What would it look like to start your day with the peace and presence of God? Set aside even five minutes each morning to start your day by grounding your being in Him.

A Prayer

As you breathe, let this prayer flow from you.
Exhale: I release anxiety.
Inhale: I embrace peace.

8

ALL BY MYSELF

Starved for God's Presence

I pulled over into a cemetery. I figured it would be a good place to weep without anyone wondering why. Of course there would be a woman under a pine tree, crying next to a tombstone!

Just a few minutes before, I'd been completely fine. I was in the grocery store ticking off my list, when just like that, I was unable to breathe. It was as if an elephant rounded the corner of the pasta aisle and parked itself on my chest. Suddenly, the pasta became blurry as the tears came up and over the mountain of emotion and charged their way down my cheeks. I had to get out of there.

I'm not sure how I managed to pay for my groceries, load them into my van, and start the car, but my impressive body carried me through like always, even as my brain went wild. It was my first panic attack, but I didn't know that's what it was at the time. All I knew was that I couldn't breathe. In an instant, just choosing a cereal from the shelf felt terrifying and overwhelming, and I wondered if anything was going to be okay again. I needed to let the tears fall, but I couldn't drive if they did.

Enter the cemetery.

I saw it, pulled in, and got out of the car. There, I let the tombstones become my touchstones, the trees my towers. They bent over me like a chorus of mothers singing over my soul. And I cried like a baby all by myself.

Just a few days before, I had gotten some news that wrecked me. The kind of news that's handed to you without a map, without hope, and without the ability to know which way is up. It was all shock and disbelief those first few days.

And now, it was tears. Liquid grief, fear, and overwhelm poured out of my body through salty tears. I let it all come. I'd learned a while ago that the only way out is through. We must give ourselves permission to travel through the tunnel of emotions and resist the urge to put up a barricade. Barricades block the process of feeling your feelings. Of welcoming them to the table. Of naming your tears and giving them value. A good twenty-minute cry has done more for me than twenty Netflix shows strung together.

I felt it all in that cemetery—the grief, despair, confusion, exhaustion, and bitterness. But underneath it all was also the faint whisper of abandonment.

Who will walk through this with me?

Will I have to walk this path alone?
Who will help me?

FEAR OF ABANDONMENT

It seems the fear of abandonment is lurking at the bottom of our souls. It sits there like the weird, hairy spiders in the basement. And then suddenly, maybe without us even knowing it's coming, we find it upon us. In our darkest fears and most difficult moments, we wonder if we'll get by all alone.

For women, the fear of abandonment comes in many shapes and sizes.

Will I ever find a partner?

If I do, will I be traded in for a younger, better woman at some point?

Will my friends leave me if I'm too much or not enough?

What if I get this job but don't have the support to succeed?

What if I say the hard and uncomfortable thing to my family and they shut me out?

Rooted in the fear of abandonment is a mistrust—a belief that God will not take care of me. That He will not tend to me like a precious sheep. That He will leave me out to pasture. That He will let go of me.

But again, the enemy spins a lie so pretty, so alluring, that we walk right toward it and take hold of it. Friend, remember that this abandonment is not from God. And believing that it is will starve us. Do not let the enemy dangle the fear of abandonment in front of you. Turn on your heels and sprint toward the truth. You are not alone and will never be. Even in the dead of winter, in the middle of the night, in the middle of a cemetery, God is there.

LED AND HELD

In Psalm 139, we see the psalmist address the fear of abandonment. In his prayer, we find a revelation—a promise meant to feed us when we're starving for the presence of God: "even there your hand shall lead me, and your right hand shall hold me" (verse 10).

Two things are true when we face feelings of abandonment: we will be led, and we will be held.

Even there, in the deepest parts of the sea.

Even there, where I am left behind, unsupported, unseen.

Even there, where I have been abused, rejected, scarred, used.

> Two things are true when we face feelings of abandonment: we will be led, and we will be held.

Even there, where it is dark and scary and there is no way out.

Even there, where the depths of grief are as dark as the bottom of the ocean.

Even there, when I don't know which way to go.

Even there, God will lead me, and God will hold me.

This is good news to the starving soul. We are not abandoned, friend. We are led, held. We are led by God into His presence and held by God in the midst of what we're facing. We are not alone because God is with us. And in knowing that to be true, we are fed.

THROUGH HIS PEOPLE

After my bitter cemetery tears, I shared my fears with two trusted friends, the conversations a day apart. One friend cried with me, held me, and prayed for me. The other friend walked next to me, deeply sighed with me, and made me laugh. But incredibly, both told me the exact same thing. They each individually said something that I didn't know I needed to hear in the middle of my fears. They said, "I'm not going anywhere. I am in this with you."

In my experience, God's presence in the face of abandonment comes through His people. His people have shown up in so many different ways in my life. I imagine (and I hope!) the same has been true for you. When the fear of abandonment rises up in our chests, it's a good practice to recount the ways God has shown us His presence through others. The body of Christ is just that—God's physical body manifested through the community of the saints. In hugs, words of encouragement, prayer, empathy, coffee drop-offs, cards, muffins, soups, lasagnas, texts, calls, hand-holding, back-porch swings, back rubs, walks, laughs—God is present in it all. We simply have to have eyes to see it.

We recently had some of our best family friends in the whole world move away. I'm not being dramatic when I tell you that it has been gut wrenching. We met this amazing family when our firstborns were babies. Since then, we've been dear friends for almost fourteen years. We have walked through it all together: babies, deaths of loved ones, schooling decisions, church community group leadership, elementary school, junior high, summer camps for our kids, church shifts and changes, preschool presidency (that was a doozy), job changes, Crohn's diagnosis, depression, anxiety, family dinners. You get the picture. My point is simply that in our lives, this family has been a presence in every moment, big and small.

When folks in our little church move on, we do an amazing job of sending them out and praying for them. Because this family was so beloved in our community, almost the entire church came forward to pray for them when they left. As I opened my mouth to pray, only tears came. Eventually, words did too. As the tears fell and I attempted to pray, I felt a compassionate hand take hold of my own. I didn't know whose hand it was; it didn't matter. What mattered was that someone held my hand. I opened my eyes to see it was another dear friend of mine, tears streaming down her face in the same way. She saw me in my fear of abandonment, in my grief, in my loss, in my prayers of blessing, in my tearful goodbye. She wanted me to know she was present with me in all of it. In that tender moment, her hands were God's hands. Her presence was God's presence with me.

I was not alone.

Friend, let me just address the difficult part of this concept: if we want to experience God's presence in the middle of our fear of abandonment, we are going to have to bravely share about the dark places with safe people. Not always easy, I know! But our people can't show up and be present in a need they don't know we have. We are going to have to let the cracks show, the tears fall, our voices quiver. We are going to have to let others into the spaces and places where we feel abandoned.

Letting others in is a great step of faith and trust in Jesus. It means you trust that He will take care of you—through His people—in your vulnerability, in your weakness, in your fragility. Is it scary? Of course! Vulnerability comes with a risk, but I promise, God will meet you in it. And the best part? He'll bring His people with Him!

FORSAKEN

Over the past several years, a dear friend of mine has uncovered abuse after abuse in her past. It was there all along, tucked away by her body so that she could survive. Through this grueling process of uncovering what has been hidden, she has lost her marriage, had several job changes, walked through the hard work of counseling, and been brought face to face with being neglected, unattended, and forsaken. But as she bravely bares her soul to people who are safe in her life, she's found glimmers of God's strength, presence, and rescue. I am a part of a small group of close friends who have knelt in prayer with her. The depth of the evil she has endured is mind boggling, and I have no idea why my friend has had to endure it. What I do know is this: Jesus understands what it's like to be forsaken.

And more than that, Jesus came for the forsaken.

The gruesome night Jesus was betrayed and abandoned by His best friends, He also felt abandoned by His Father. Having endured excruciating humiliation and pain hanging on the cross, Jesus cried out the words of a familiar psalm: "My God, my God, why have you forsaken me? Why are you so far from saving me, from the words of my groaning?" (Psalm 22:1).

Other translations use the word "abandoned" in place of "forsaken." There on the cross, Jesus felt abandoned. He felt forsaken. Forgotten. Alone. Helpless. Left without the presence of His good, good Father by His side. If we're honest, I think we'd all say we know what Jesus felt here. Because we've felt it too! In our deepest moments of pain, sometimes we wonder if God has left us. Have we been abandoned? Forsaken? Left to starve without the presence of God to feed us?

In the very middle of this emotional darkness for Jesus, an interesting correlation happens. Jesus gets thirsty. His spiritual starvation becomes mirrored by His physical thirst. He is starving in every single way: body, mind, and soul.

> After this, Jesus, knowing that all was now finished, said (to fulfill the Scripture), "I thirst." A jar full of sour wine stood there, so they put a sponge full of the sour wine on a hyssop branch and held it to his mouth. When Jesus had received the sour wine, he said, "It is finished," and he bowed his head and gave up his spirit.
> JOHN 19:28-30

Jesus felt abandoned in every one of His senses. The deep lack of spiritual satiation was felt throughout His whole being. Jesus was spiritually bereft and physically parched. And then, He gave up His spirit. The darkness had overcome.

Or so it seemed.

Tim Keller teaches, "Jesus was abandoned so we never would be; Jesus thirsted in His abandonment so we would not thirst in ours."[1] And friend, I believe this is true to my very core. I don't know what darkness has overcome you. What abandonment you have experienced. What thirst you have so deep in your soul that your whole body feels it. What demons sit on your doorstep to try to tell you that you're worthless to God. I don't know why you feel forsaken.

But what I do know is that Jesus' story—the story of our Savior—tells us there is always hope. Light always comes after darkness. Morning always follows night. Death has been defeated. God's abiding presence is with us—in us— even in our abandonment. Even there, in our forsaken place, God is taking our abandonment and making beauty out of the ashes.

AT DAWN

Let's remember what happens after Jesus is forsaken:

> At dawn on the first day of the week, Mary
> Magdalene and the other Mary went to look at
> the tomb.
>
> There was a violent earthquake, for an angel of the
> Lord came down from heaven and, going to the tomb,
> rolled back the stone and sat on it. . . .
>
> The angel said to the women, "Do not be afraid,
> for I know that you are looking for Jesus, who was
> crucified. He is not here; he has risen, just as he said.
> Come and see the place where he lay."
>
> MATTHEW 28:1-2; 5-6, NIV

This passage includes two important words: at dawn. Light had indeed come. The darkness had subsided. Healing had come. An earthquake had come. Angels had come. And a resurrection had come.

Dawn always comes after the darkness.

Dawn is coming, dear one.

Hold on to that hope as you cry in a cemetery and wonder if God is with you.

Hold on to the promise that God leads you and holds you, even there.

Hold on to the truth that God wants to replace our fear of abandonment with His Spirit abiding in us.

Hold on to the hand that has reached out for yours.

Hold on to the saints who have walked before you in the dark, dark night.

Hold on to the stories of those who have come out of it to witness a breathtaking sunrise.

Hold on to the truth that you are not forsaken; Jesus made sure of that.

Hold on, dear one.

Dawn is coming.

THROUGH HIS SPIRIT

We know God's presence through community, but we also know His presence through His Spirit. Part of the gift that Jesus gave in the dawn after His death is the assurance that we would never be abandoned, even though sometimes we feel it so deeply. That gift comes in the form of His Spirit—the presence of God living inside of us. But that Spirit only came after the dark night—after Jesus' crucifixion and abandonment. After Jesus' resurrection, He appeared to His disciples to give them a parting gift: "Jesus said to them again, 'Peace be with you. As the Father has sent me, even so I am sending you.' And when he had said this, he breathed on them and said to them, 'Receive the Holy Spirit'" (John 20:21-22).

The gift of this Spirit inside of us assures us we are never, ever alone. Even when our feelings are desperately trying to change the facts, they cannot. The truth remains the same: God is with us in every single place. Where can we go from His Spirit? Where can we flee from His presence? (See Psalm 139.) Even there, when we feel utterly alone, He is with us. Inside of us. Leading and holding us.

In the weeks and months after recalling my own sexual abuse as a child, I spent a lot of time in counseling walking through those hurts. I'm sure you can image how dark and difficult that season was. I'm sure you can understand how often I wanted to believe I'd been forsaken, forgotten, left alone to manage the dark night of this pain. One day, I found myself on the floor of my room with my Bible open, asking God for healing and freedom from the abuse. I was at a really low, depressed point. I hadn't really even sat down to process through the actual event yet. It felt too scary to bring up. It was too much to think about again by myself. But from my counselor's recommendation and the Spirit's leading, I went back to that night in my mind.

As I did, one of the craziest and most powerful visuals came to mind. I imagined myself back in the place I was abused, but this time, as I saw myself, a fresh wind and new power came over the house. In my mind's eye, I saw the roof come off, the walls fold down, and the abuser unable to get into the room where I lay innocently sleeping. Surrounding the house was a hot lava moat, a thundering voice, and a strong sense that the most powerful Being in the universe was clearing the way to get to me. He was coming with lightning, thunder, and hail to pick me up out of this pit of despair and bring me to a safe place.

You might think I was frightened by this whole thing, but I wasn't. I was watching the rescue of a sweet little girl. I saw protection. I saw fierce anger at the abuser. I saw provision. I saw a new, different story than the one I had lived. Warm tears streamed down my face. I was safe. No one could get to me. I was not abandoned; I was not forsaken. No, by God's powerful Spirit, I was rescued.

It all felt really familiar, almost like I had imagined it all before. And then it hit me: it was Psalm 18! There on the floor, I couldn't flip to it fast enough. Psalm 18 has long been beloved to me. I've returned to it in many seasons of my life when I have felt depressed, abandoned, alone, forsaken, forgotten, or unseen. I'd spent so much time reading and meditating on it, it felt like my own psalm. That day, I read it with fresh eyes.

> He sent from on high, he took me;
>> he drew me out of many waters.
> He rescued me from my strong enemy
>> and from those who hated me,
>>> for they were too mighty for me.
> They confronted me in the day of my calamity,

> but the LORD was my support.
> He brought me out into a broad place;
> > he rescued me, because he delighted in me.

PSALM 18:16-19

Again, the tears couldn't be stopped. Only this time, they were tears of relief, rescue, and safety. These weren't tears of abandonment; these were tears of being held. Tears of the reminder that God's Spirit was there with me and fighting for me, even there. Tears not of starvation, but of satisfaction.

The Spirit gave me that picture in my mind that day. The Spirit heard those desperate prayers for freedom and answered them with a new image, a new story, a new freedom. It was the reframing of a memory—a gift I'll never get over. The Spirit of God replaced my starvation for His presence in the worst moment of my life with a powerful picture to remind me that His rescuing presence was with me then and remains with me now.

Friend, that presence is with you today too. God wants to replace your abandonment with His presence. He wants you to see that He is with you through the people He's put around you and the Spirit that lives inside of you. In His presence, He wants you to be fully fed, fully nourished, and fully satisfied.

> **In His presence, you are fully fed, fully nourished, and fully satisfied.**

May we spend time remembering God is with us. May we commit to telling the truth in the face of feelings. May we practice turning our attention to God and listening for His healing voice.

May we feel His presence even there.

A Practice

This week, choose a spot and time to practice meditating in the presence of God. Remember, this is simply coming before the Lord. You want to hear from God and be reminded of His presence. So, give yourself space to do just that. And it may be very difficult at first. You may have lists flying in your mind and anxiety and overwhelming thoughts. Ask the Lord to quiet your mind and consider His Word in places where it wants to wander. Sit in God's presence and truth as a reminder that you have never been and will never be abandoned or forsaken.

A Prayer

Start with your palms down as a symbolic gesture to release your cares and concerns to God. Be specific about what exactly has left you feeling forsaken in this moment. Start with something like this:

God, I give you these cares and concerns. I am laying down the things that have left me feeling forsaken and forgotten. I acknowledge that I feel abandoned in this season.

Then, turn your palms up in a posture to receive. Ask God to help you receive the gift of His presence with you. Start with something like this:

God, I receive Your presence. I know that You are with me. I know You have been with me always. Help me to see You in the situations I feel alone or abandoned in. Show me Your presence with me even there.

9

BROWNIES AND BIBLE STUDY

Starved for Identity

He told me I could bring the brownies.

To Bible study.

As his Bible study coleader.

Apparently, he decided he would take care of the Bible study part and I could take care of the brownie part. Funny, I don't remember "brownies" being in the phrase "Bible study" (because it's not!). Yet somehow, here we were.

Leaves fell in a dreamy pattern around me as I opened the door to the Bowling Green State University student center. A mix of hope and anxiety pulsed through the room as college men and women talked about starting fall classes. Students were exchanging high fives and welcome-back hugs, off-loading book bags in between classes, coaxing vending machines to release candy bars and caffeinated drinks. Eager for what God had for me, I was excited to sit down and plan the Bible study lessons for the college ministry I was involved in, but with that opening statement from my coleader, something shifted.

We'd been paired up to lead a coed Bible study in one of the residence halls that year. I was a senior in college and had been studying and teaching the Bible for a few years at this point, mentoring women, leading in a variety of ways, and even teaching at the weekly meeting (which typically had been reserved for the staff team). I was anticipating the adventure of my last year in college with this ministry I had grown to love. Eager and energized, I was ready to be used by God. My coleader was a first-year intern on the campus ministry staff team, and the greater powers of the staff team thought we would be a good match. A green staff guy and an energetic senior college girl—I can see why they thought this could work. But what looks good on paper can sometimes fall apart in practice.

I couldn't put words to what rose up inside of me when he politely told me I could contribute little more than dessert to our study. A cocktail of disappointment, offense, shame, uselessness, anger, and frustration sloshed around my soul. What was I supposed to do with this statement? I felt a clear call on my life to teach the Bible, something that others who were older and wiser had affirmed. But in this moment, I felt discouraged, unseen, and sidelined. I was told to bring the brownies when all I wanted to do was bring the Word.

Even more perplexing was what I had repeatedly seen modeled with my own two eyes: a co-led ministry with a man and a woman serving together as equals. I saw a generous shared plate of responsibilities, microphone time, teaching, and mutual submission among the men and women in that ministry. I think that's what made his one little sentence in the corner of the student center—said as casually as a comment about the weather—so completely disorienting.

It's been twenty years since that life-changing exchange. Twenty years of continuing to hear a lot of ideas about how I ought to spend my time, use my gifts, and act as a woman in ministry. Twenty years of cradling that way-down-deep knowledge about what I was made for but wrestling with confidence, submission, pride, position, titles, calling, fear, boldness, opinions, people-pleasing, and the church at large. Twenty years of flipping back and forth with this reality in my mind.

I was made to write and speak and lead; I was a woman in a place where men were in charge.

WHO WILL YOU LISTEN TO?

Decades later, God continues to remind me of something I need—something we all need. It's vital to our growth, to our confidence, and to following Jesus. It's what will keep us from wilting and starving. It's what will certainly replenish our dry and thirsty souls.

We need to listen to God first.

We need to listen to God first.

We need to let God tell us who we are and what He's called us to do. We need to let God's voice speak into our identity. To talk to Him about taking off the labels everyone else has given us—or to keep the ones that fit what He intends. Let's practice listening to His voice first (and sometimes exclusively!). Because, friend, allowing others to speak into the core of who we are and what we do—without taking these things to God first—will starve us.

Yes, God uses community to encourage us and to affirm us. We need others to speak into our lives, to call us out and up. Community is vital (I have a whole chapter coming on this!). But we also have an enemy who seeks to destroy us and lie to us. The only way to know the difference between the two? By taking our identity to God, first. By taking someone's words over us to Him, first. By taking it all to the One who made us and knows us, first. That will allow us to flourish.

Stepping outside the student center building that day (after I muttered a "sounds good" that I obviously didn't mean), I put my left hand to my head and sensed a sudden need for water. My mouth was as dry as the Sahara in summer. I looked around, but I don't know what I was hoping to find. Maybe someone to verify that I was more than a brownie-bringer? Maybe just a way to collect my thoughts and find a drinking fountain? Maybe the will to just walk away, forget my teaching gifts, and accept my lot as the Bible study baker?

This plan did not sound good. In fact, it sounded terrible. For one, I didn't even like baking back then; I had burned my fair share of frozen pizzas. On a very basic and fundamental level, putting me in charge of brownies was a bad idea. And "the" brownies? As if every Bible study required them? Why must there be sugar at every Christian event? And why do we insist on asking the girls to bring it?!

But there was obviously more to the issue than brownies. Yes, I was a younger, less experienced Bible teacher than my coleader. But the truth was that God seemed to use my little Bible studies to bring college women closer to Him. The truth was that my coleader didn't think I had what it would take. The truth was that what he said was offensive, hurtful, misogynistic, short-sighted, patriarchal, and arrogant. The truth was that I was hurt. The truth was that I had to figure out what to do with the truth.

I had to decide whose voice I was going to listen to.

SCARS

I realize that much more hurtful, damaging, and traumatic words have been penned or spewed at you, at me, at us. We all have our "bring the brownies" moments. Moments when we feel belittled and unseen. We have been categorized, abused, or used as pawns in a larger religious or otherwise chess game. We have been spit on, cursed at, shoved around, told to go back to where we came from. We have been called derogatory names based on the glorious and rich color of our skin, or the lovely shape of our eyes, or the gender that was carefully crafted by our Creator in our mothers' wombs. We have had moments in our stories that have left scars.

But the truth? The absolute healing truth of it all? The truth that defeats the lies? The only scars that truly define us are the ones Jesus has.

The only scars that truly define us are the ones Jesus has.

I don't say this lightly, friend. I am by no means belittling the experiences, the words, the weight placed on us by others. I'm not brushing past what these things have done to starve us of our true identity. I'm not glossing over the healing we need in order to be nourished in the truth of who we are again.

What I am saying is that our scars are not the sum of who we are. Jesus' scars seal our identity. His scars say we are accepted, we are loved, we are free, and we are His. His scars say we are so incredibly valuable to Him that He would die for us. His scars say that though the world wants to tell us otherwise, we are wildly loved, valuable, and necessary, to the point of death.

Remember how the father felt about his prodigal son who had taken his entire inheritance, packed his bags, skipped town, and spent every last dollar? How his father was on the front porch day after day, raising his hand to his forehead and peering into the distance? Waiting and watching to restore his son to himself? When the day came, he finally saw his son. His whole entire being was filled with compassion at the very sight of him. Remember how the father grabbed his long robes and hiked them up in such an undignified manner it would make others blush? And how he leaped down the front steps and broke into an all-out sprint toward his boy? Remember how, when he reached his son, he hugged him with a great bear hug that only a father can give?

In that story, we don't see just a father running to his lost son. We see our Father running to us, seeing our scars with compassionate eyes, and reminding us who we are.

His.

The father in the story bore the brunt of the inheritance that was lost. He took the debt and absorbed it. And not only did he absorb it, he then took *more* of what was his—his clothes, his ring, his shoes—and gave them to his son again. He gave *more*. He slaughtered a cow for a feast. He paid for a party in the wake of wasted wealth. There was nothing he wouldn't have done to celebrate the return of his beloved son.

And friend, this is what God's extravagant love does for us. Whether we come to Him with scars we've caused or scars we've received. Whether we have bought—hook, line, and sinker—what everyone else has said about us. Whether we are unable to untangle our identity from our work or the applause or the praise or the harsh words. Whether we struggle greatly with believing we are worthy to be called God's. The truth is, His scars are the source of our identity. They are the proof of His love for us in the face of such hurt and pain.

And this is what we are starving for—the restorative love of God that defines who we are and whose we are. The love that lets us take off the chains of the approval of others. The love that lets us shed the shackles of the opinions of others. The love that gives us our identity.

THE PRACTICE OF PRAYER

So how do we get there? Yes, you guessed it: we practice! Allowing our identity to be nourished by God alone isn't going to come naturally. What comes naturally? Lies and arrows and slurs and pain. If we leave it there, we're ultimately going to starve. But if we practice consistently rooting ourselves in who God says we are, we'll find satisfaction.

The practice that best helps us replace the opinions of others with the opinions of God is prayer. We talk to God, and God talks to us. We spend time with our Maker; we let Him tell us who He made us to be.

Now, I'll just come out and tell you that I am not good at listening to the quiet whisper of God. I am far better at listening to the loud applause or noisy opinions of others. But I'm practicing. I am finding ways to connect to God's voice and disconnect from others' voices. I am finding what works and what doesn't. Just the way you do with a good friend or your spouse, I am finding a rhythm of communication between my Father and myself. And in that rhythm, I'm finding peace in who I really am.

I'm finding my identity.

One of the ways I listen to God's voice is by choosing a song that tells about who God is and who I am. I walk, and I listen, and I sing, and I pray. I let the truth wash over my soul. When the soundtrack of someone else's voice is stuck on repeat, it's time for a new soundtrack, and an actual song can do wonders. Songs can act as prayers. They can help us meet with God. They can remind us of what is true.

Recently I had a full lineup of teaching and travel all in one week. One of the places I'd be speaking had one of the largest crowds I had ever taught in front of. The days leading up to this full week, I found myself rehearsing my talks in the car, the shower, the garden. Ever so slowly, the pressure to perform, to prove, to gain the approval of others crept in like a quiet lion in the tall grasses looking for her prey. My thoughts turned to the need to teach perfectly so that I could win everyone over and prove that women can indeed preach. Clearly, the request for brownies almost two decades ago was still hovering over me!

Eventually, my thoughts about who I was shifted to who I wasn't. I wasn't ordained. I wasn't theologically trained. I wasn't carrying the title "pastor" with my name. Who was I to teach? I only had a handful of seminary classes taken over a decade in my pocket. So if I got up there, I had to crush it. There was no room for error. I needed to prove that women can be called by God and gifted to share His message. It felt like the weight of all women in ministry was riding on my shoulders. Our identity as a whole was at stake.

Talk about starving!

I needed a new conversation in my head, and I needed Jesus to help me get there. As I was reaching higher levels of anxiety, the lyrics to the song "The Blessing" came to mind.

The Lord bless you
And keep you
Make His face shine upon you . . .

It was a song we had sung in church about six months before that. Did God want me to listen to it now? Was this song an invitation to meet God on a walk and let Him talk to me? It's happened enough times that this felt like Him to me.

So, I set my kids up with a show and snacks, I popped my earbuds in to find the song, and I went for a walk around the block. If you had been anywhere near me on that walk, you would have thought a dam had opened up inside of me. With Kari Jobe singing those words over me, the pressure to perform broke, and I started to cry Hoover Dam tears. Each tear seemed to carry a lie away from my heart, away from my mind, and away from my soul. Prove, push, please, perform, perfect—they all fell to the ground in saltwater droplets that day. I released the fears, the comments, and the labels given to me over the years. I let go of the words spoken years ago by members of my congregation who didn't think women should teach. I was the only woman who had ever taught at my church, so this wasn't some general idea. It was personal because it was about me. They thought I should not teach, and that alone had been starving me of my true identity. If I wanted to step into my God-given calling and God-given identity, I had to let it go.

After opening my hands on my walk, pretending and practicing the act of letting all the identities others have given me fall to the ground, I now had open hands to receive God's identity for me. I could embrace the blessing that was being sung over me—the blessing of God's face turned toward me, in love, delight, and affection. If not one person said one positive thing to me after I taught, I was going to be okay. I was still going to be enough. It was enough to be faithful to the assignment given to me by my good Father. It was enough to enjoy God as I encouraged people from up front. It was enough to do it with God alone. It was enough to be blessed by God before I spoke one word in front of anyone else. It was enough to just walk and let God's truth sing over me. It was enough to receive a song that brought healing and wholeness, identity and security.

Am I forever fixed by that walk? I wish! But it's walks like this that build up the memories I have with God to draw on when the lies come. When the insecurity tries to bury me alive. When the brownie narrative comes back. I can try a walk, a song, a good cry to tap into the truth and rewire my thinking. It's all in the practice.

I AM...

In the book of Numbers, the Lord directed Moses and Aaron to bless the Israelites:

Say to them:

"The LORD bless you
    and keep you;
the LORD make his face shine on you
    and be gracious to you;
the LORD turn his face toward you
    and give you peace."

So they will put my name on the Israelites, and I will bless them.

NUMBERS 6:23-27, NIV

Did you catch the very last part?
"They will put my name on the Israelites."
If this isn't an identity, I don't know what is. God's name on them, on us, on anyone who follows Him. We are His, and

He is ours. We are clearly labeled and marked by our Father: *Mine*. This is one of the hallmark moments of our identity.

It's described again in the very last book of the Bible, when Jesus comes back to put everything to right. There we find a beautiful description of our identity sealed forever by His name upon us. No longer will we question who we are, or how God feels about us, or who made us with loving hands. No longer will we starve. Instead, we'll be sealed, nourished, and marked by who we are in Christ. On that day, "His servants shall serve Him. They shall see His face, and His name shall be on their foreheads" (Revelation 22:3-4, NKJV).

I am not a brownie baker.

I am not a slave to others' opinions.

I am not responsible to prove women can do things in God's Kingdom.

I am a beloved daughter of the Most High King.

I am free from the opinion of others and blessed by my Father.

I am responsible only for being faithful to what my Father has given me, no more, no less.

This is who I am, stamped on my forehead by the great I Am. This is the place my soul can rest. This is my identity.

This is *your* identity.

THE LORD'S PRAYER

Friend, let's be honest here: there are days I don't have a prayer to pray. I don't have a song to sing, a word to say, a thought to give to the Lord. Maybe you know exactly how this feels. If you do, then we're in good company. Jesus' own disciples ran into this word block themselves. They, too, looked at Jesus, feeling lost about how to pray, and said, "Teach us!"

So Jesus did. He gave a very simple, very profound prayer that has been memorized and shared for centuries. (Turns out, templates are really helpful when we don't know what in the world we are doing!) Jesus gave them what is now called the Lord's Prayer.

> Our Father in heaven,
>> may your name be kept holy.
> May your Kingdom come soon.
> May your will be done on earth,
>> as it is in heaven.
> Give us today the food we need,
> and forgive us our sins,
>> as we have forgiven those who sin against us.
> And don't let us yield to temptation,
>> but rescue us from the evil one.
>
> MATTHEW 6:9-13, NLT

When we can't find our own words to pray, the Lord's Prayer is where we can look. In Jesus' words, we find six themes that will help us shape our prayers when our souls desperately need to speak to the Father. These are the themes we can use:

Father: You are my good Father, and I have a family.
Worship: You, alone, are worthy of my worship.
Heaven: Let Your Kingdom invade our world, our city,
    our neighborhood, our hearts.

Provision: I trust You to provide everything I need.

Forgiveness: We humbly come in need of forgiveness and in need of extending it to others.

Rescue: We need Your strength and Your protection from our enemy.

When I feel lost for words, I come back to these themes with two questions: What does my heart need right now? What part of my identity feels shaken?

Do I need to know I have a Father who loves me?

Do I need to turn away from my self-worship and worship God?

Do I need to pray for God's Kingdom to flourish right here?

Do I need to remember that God will take care of me?

Do I need to confess my sin and find forgiveness, or come to forgive another?

Do I need to know God's rescuing strength today?

Jesus has not left us without help or without hope. He has given us a way to pray, a way to come, a way to commune with Him so we can embrace who we are and who God is. May these words be the call back to connecting with our Father and finding our identity in Him alone. May we be people who replace the opinions of others with God's approval, acceptance, and affection. May we pray through tears and songs, through freedom and fear. May we practice praying the truth of who God is and who we are, letting go of the lies. May we be nourished in the truth of who we really are.

A Practice

Prayer can come with groans and sighs (Romans 8:26-27), through songs and dancing (as in Psalm 145), or through preset words (the Lord's Prayer). This week, choose a prayer practice. Is it a walk and a song? Is it very slowly saying each word of the Lord's Prayer? Is it choosing one of the themes in the Lord's Prayer and talking to Jesus about it? Whatever it is for you, make this practice of prayer a habit this week, asking God to remind you who you are in Him.

A Prayer

As you breathe, let this prayer flow from you.

Exhale: I release the words and opinions of others who want to shape my identity.

Inhale: I take in the truth of who You say I am, Father. I find my identity in You.

10

PLAYING THE BLAME GAME

Starved for Confession

I couldn't stop highlighting that stupid book.

I hated how much it was speaking to me. Surely this wasn't describing me? This was just a case study, not my own life, right?

Do I do this?

Believe this?

Live like this?

Several years ago, I noticed my short fuse was getting shorter. I was snapping at my kids, angry at my life, and frustrated at my circumstances. The endless mundane tasks of motherhood—the feeling that I was trapped and stuck in the depressed hopelessness of another Groundhog Day— were adding up. I was a constantly boiling teakettle, ready any minute to blow the whistle and pour out scalding hot water on whomever was closest.

My anger was an issue, and I needed help.

I found myself angry at little things, big things, any things, really. My temper was rising uncontrollably at the drop of a hat. Something needed to give before I gave way to more pain and hurt poured down upon my kids and my husband. The people closest to me were paying the price for the work I had refused to do, and now it was time to lift up the lid and see what was building underneath it.

That's how I found this life-changing and incredibly convicting little book, *Controlling Your Anger before It Controls You*. You guys, it wasn't messing around. It also seemed like it had won the "Least Likely to Be Read at a Coffeeshop for the World to See and Judge Your Issues" award. So, I made the choice to read in the comfort of my own home, where I promptly found myself underlining entirely too much.

In one particular case study, "Colleen" had some key assumptions about herself. Those assumptions led to disappointment and disappointment led to anger. Here's a snapshot of what I underlined from her story:

- *I need to be perfect to be happy.* Colleen believed an ordered world would be a happy world, so she set out to control as many people and events as she could. This stranglehold of control was one reason her marriage failed.
- *When I am upset, it is the responsibility of others to comfort me.* . . . Colleen came to rely on the intervention of others to handle her own discomfort. . . .

- *When others harm me, it is intentional.* When injured, Colleen learned to lash out in anger. It was difficult for her to believe in and allow for the mistakes of others, especially when she held herself to such a rigid standard of perfection. . . .
- *When I harm others, it is a mistake.* Because of her need to see herself as perfect for her sense of self-worth, Colleen was loathe to admit she did anything worthy of forgiveness.[1]

I could go on and on, but I'll stop here and spare you the gory details. Every page turned was like a horrifying glimpse into the mirror of my own life. I wanted to slam the book closed and run for the hills. I wasn't *this* bad, was I?

A few pages later, a line at the end of this particular section jumped off the page, demanding my attention: "The only way for Colleen to get control over her life was to realize she had that control all along . . . by accepting the responsibility, she rediscovered the control."

THE BLAME GAME

Anyone else find themselves routinely playing the blame game when it comes to their anger? Sure, our fuses may be short, but that's not our fault entirely, is it? People are forcing us to react this way. Circumstances are demanding our anger. We can't help it, can we?

Well, as it turns out, we can.

And this takes us right back to where it all began—back to the Garden. For crying out loud! We could circle back endlessly to Eden and find sources of starvation at every turn. We swallowed a whole host of lies in one juicy bite, one of which being this:

You don't have any control, so blame everyone else for the mess you've made. You aren't responsible. Everyone else did this to you. You were just in the wrong place at the wrong time. You're off the hook. You're a victim.

Anybody else resonating just a little too closely with that line of thought? I know I am! I have been the queen of the blame game when it comes to my anger. And what I'm beginning to realize is that's exactly how the Snake intended it to be. Just look at how it went down in Genesis:

> He [God] said, "Who told you that you were naked? Have you eaten from the tree that I commanded you not to eat from?"
>
> The man said, "The woman you put here with me—she gave me some fruit from the tree, and I ate it."
>
> Then the Lord God said to the woman, "What is this you have done?"
>
> The woman said, "The serpent deceived me, and I ate."
>
> GENESIS 3:11-13, NIV

This, my friend, is where the blame game began.

The man blames the woman.

The woman blames the Snake.

The Snake slithers away smiling, leaving a mess in his wake.

Later, Jesus refers to the Snake as the "Father of Lies" (John 8:44). And that's exactly who he is! The Snake has no truth in him, and his goal is to get us to forsake the truth about God and our world. And of course, to lie to ourselves by playing a few rounds of the blame game in our own lives.

It's not my fault.

I was pushed to this point.

I'm hurt too.

You don't understand what I'm dealing with.

I can't help myself.

Again, if this sounds familiar to you, you're in great company here with me! But friend, just because we've made the blame game a way of life before doesn't mean we can't choose a different way going forward. The lies, the anger, the blowups, the lack of control—it's starving us. And the only thing that can nourish us back to life—back to self-control—is the truth.

TRUTH-TELLING

Of course, actually accepting the truth about ourselves, our sin, our mistakes, our flaws, our failures, and our responsibilities can be incredibly difficult. We have been lied to and deceived since the very beginning. We have been told we're fine—that it's everyone else's fault. We have used blame to shift the responsibility and ownership. We've been making scapegoats since goats were created. We have been pointing the finger at everyone else except us. And slowly, it's eating us alive.

The lack of ownership in our lives is bringing nothing more than frustration, anger, disunity, racism, depression, anxiety, and hopelessness. But truth-telling brings us shalom.

Truth-telling is the way of Jesus—who is the Way, the Truth, and the Life. Truth-telling is life giving, even if it means admitting ting the worst about ourselves. Truth-telling is for our healing, our integrated living, our wholeness. Truth-telling will bring us out of the dark night of starvation and into the light of nourishment.

> **Truth-telling is life giving, even if it means admitting the worst about ourselves.**

Light exposes what is real. Lies can stay alive in the dark, but once the light is flipped on, we're able to see everything for what it actually is. That's where truth is found: in the light.

At the beginning of John 8, we encounter a woman caught in the very act of adultery. She is dropped in front of Jesus as he's teaching in the Temple. The scribes and Pharisees expose her sin publicly and ask Jesus if she should be stoned. (Mind you, the man is left alone, not also publicly humiliated, but that's another story!) They attempt to shine a light on her shame, but Jesus, being compassionate and merciful when faced with the truth of what she was involved in, uses His light in a different way. He swivels the flashlight on the souls of those who exposed her, reminding them of their own sins that need to be dragged into the light along with the woman's. One by one, they leave, unable to throw a stone at her under the weight of their own shame.

When all is said and done, Jesus is left to deal with the woman. Rather than condemn her, He chooses compassion. He chooses light. He chooses truth. He tells the crowd, "I am the light of the world. Whoever follows me will not walk in darkness, but will have the light of life" (John 8:12, NIV).

It's a statement for this woman, yes, but it's a statement for us today, too. Jesus is the light. He is the only One who can shine the light of truth over our deepest, darkest places. He is the only One who can change us.

Light, truth-telling, and confession pour water on our dry souls. We are so hungry to live integrated lives—to stop living fractured and splintered lives. We long to be free of saying one thing and believing another. We long to come out from hiding in the dark and to be free in the light. We hurt others, but believe we are perfect. We make mistakes but blame others. We live frustrated and upset but think it's someone else's job to make us happy.

And we are starving.

But truth brings nourishment. It brings shalom, wholeheartedness, and healing. Truth brings hope, joy, and freedom. Truth changes everything for our hungry and heavy souls.

The good news is we have Jesus to be our guide here. Because honest confession isn't easy. Truth-telling is not for the faint of heart! Thank God for a Savior to go before us in this!

In the book of Luke, we see Jesus telling a tale of two men. Both come to the Temple to pray. Both come to the place where God dwelt. Both come toward His presence. But one was honest about his sins, and one was not. So in the end, one was made right with God, and one was not.

As the story closes, Jesus reminds those listening (and us today!) of this truth: "All those who exalt themselves will be humbled, and those who humble themselves will be exalted" (Luke 18:14, NIV).

Isn't this so interesting? The world wants us to believe that lifting ourselves up, justifying our behavior, never being at fault will be what saves us. If we exalt ourselves, we're doing it right, right? But Jesus gives us a different way—a better way. He reminds us that those who humble themselves are the ones who will be lifted up in His Kingdom. And friend, what's more humbling than truth-telling? When we choose to tell the truth to ourselves and others, we're ultimately choosing the way that will exalt us, heal us, and lift us up in the Kingdom of God.

> When we choose to tell the truth to ourselves and others, we're ultimately choosing the way of healing.

Our ability to self-justify is so masterful. We often deceive ourselves and believe we are not in need of daily mercy, grace, and forgiveness. We are fantastic finger-pointers and brilliant blamers. But feasting on self-justification is the fastest way to starve.

Truth-telling will set us free.

One of my children recently tripped and fell. When they did, they immediately yelled at their sibling, who was minding their own business in the next room. My child, lying on the ground with their pride and perfectionism bruised, reached for the blame tool. Surely it wasn't their fault that they tripped over their own two feet! This must have been a result of something another child did to them. Rather than face the truth of their own clumsiness, they chose the life of self-deception.

As I watched this unfold, I realized I was watching myself. I, too, want others to rescue me, others to own my problems, others to take care of my bruises. I have blamed my husband when my computer fails me. I have accused my children of making my life hard. I have stewed in anger when my comfort is compromised. I have told myself lies about how the world works, assuming it should bend for me.

And if I wanted that to change, I had to tell the truth to myself. I had to start unlearning the deception from the Snake, the lies I tell myself, and the tools given to me by a culture of self-justification.

DUMP MY CUP

One of the practices that has helped me immensely in this unlearning has been to "dump my cup." Author Paul Tripp points out that whatever is inside of our cup is what will spill out of it.[2] If we walk around our house with hot coffee in our cup, when someone bumps into us, hot coffee will spill out. Of course, I could easily blame the one bumping into me for the hot coffee that spilled out. But in reality, because *I* had hot coffee in my cup, hot coffee spilled out scalding the one *I* bumped.

In the same way, if I walk around with bitterness, entitlement, and frustration in my cup, that is what will spill out on anyone who metaphorically bumps into me. If that's what's brewing in me, that's what's going to come out. But if I have a mug filled with love, peace, and joy? Well, then the person I bumped into will be smothered in love, peace, and joy. They'll be better after their interaction with me.

To make sure I only carry the things in my cup that will better myself and others, I routinely have to practice looking inside my cup and dumping out the stuff that doesn't come from God.

The anger.

The bitterness.

The fear.

The comparison.

The entitlement.

The greed.

The anxiety.

Everything must go! Sometimes I even take a pretend cup and pretend pour it out in my kitchen to the Lord. This is what the psalmist tells us to do: "Trust in him at all times, you people; pour out your hearts to him, for God is our refuge" (Psalm 62:8, NIV).

While I whine and complain and tell my good Father everything, He takes what's in my cup. And then, I ask Him to fill my cup with what's His.

His goodness.

His love.

His joy.

His hope.

His compassion.

His grace.

This practice helps me take ownership and responsibility of what's in my cup, and that makes room to fill it again with what comes from the Lord.

As a parent, I try to practice growth mindset phrases with my children, encouraging them that we're not just stuck with what we're born with; we can continue to develop our talents and abilities. As I was researching phrases to write out and tape to our wall (and possibly tape to our foreheads), I was caught off guard by one particular growth mindset phrase.

I can solve my problems.

This simple phrase tears off the shiny veneer of perfectionism. It asks us to admit we have problems. We are not perfect; we are not problem-free. And if we want to dump the stuff that isn't serving us out of our cups, we first have to acknowledge that it's there. This phrase empowers us to do just that! Self-deception leaves no room for duality, for both/and, for holding two different things in one hand. It creates a fixed mindset that says, "You are this way, cemented in, and that's just how it is." But in this tiny phrase, I found encouragement to choose a different mindset—one that makes room for both the problem and the solution.

I have problems, AND I am empowered to solve them.

I am a sinner, AND I am forgiven.

I have weaknesses, AND I also have strength.

I make messes, AND I can clean them up.

The Snake wants us to believe we are not responsible for our actions or our problems or our sin. He wants us to believe we are beyond grace in either direction, with our pride or our self-pity. He wants us to believe we are perfect, so we don't need grace. He wants us to believe there are problems around us, but they are not ours. And even if they were our problems, we would not be able to fix them. He wants us to believe we are broken, and therefore we cannot also be beautiful. He wants us to believe we are helpless and hopeless.

When we're dumping our cup, we're pouring out the lies, the problems, the deception that isn't serving us.

We're acknowledging the problems and our power to solve them with the help of God. We're starting the practice of confession.

THE PRACTICE OF CONFESSION

So how do we embrace a mindset that is fixed on God's grace? We practice confessing the truth and embracing the power we have from God. What would it look like if we woke up each morning and started with a mindset centered on spiritual growth? If we recited the truth before anything else? If we confessed our need for God's help before making any other moves?

This practice of confession has worked wonders for me. I think it might do the same for you! I've written out a five-fold confession for us both—something to give us the truth and grace of being human beings, made and loved by God.

God made me, loves me, and enjoys restoring me back to what He intended me to be (see 2 Corinthians 5:17).

The truth is that I am sinful and broken AND God is gracious and forgiving (see 1 John 1:9).

The truth is I am messy and self-serving AND God's Spirit empowers me to make it right and serve others (see Galatians 5:22-24).

The truth is I hurt people AND I can help heal relationships through asking forgiveness and rebuilding trust (see Psalm 103:12).

The truth is I make mistakes AND God is not done with

me yet. He will continue to grow me up through my mistakes and failures like a good, good Father (see Philippians 1:6).

If we practiced stating this five-fold reality of who we are and who God is in response, I think grace would abound for us and for others. The more we pay compassionate attention to ourselves—gently accepting the truth of our broken but bright reality—the more we will pay compassionate attention to those closest to us and around us.

The more we'll be nourished by the practice of confession.

ACCEPTING RESPONSIBILITY

"I feel like you're mad at me. You're yelling at me. I am just trying to help you."

Gently but firmly, my husband spoke this truth to me. By doing so, he also threw a wrench in the well-oiled marriage system we had built, which looked like this: a problem arose in my life. I tried to fix it myself. If that didn't work, I got frustrated, I called my husband to fix it, and I spoke to him in a very frustrated manner. I expected him to drop everything and fix it, and he usually would.

I was a real peach.

But this time, my husband was done. He was ready to expose this pattern in our relationship to prove that maybe this machine wasn't as well-oiled as I wanted to believe.

Once again, I couldn't figure out how to do something on my computer. My husband works on a computer all day long, and I was sure he would put everything down to help me so that I could move on with my day. But when he did, I yelled at him. Again. And he was tired of it.

Instead of acknowledging the weight of his words and accepting any actual responsibility, I took a different route.

"I'm not mad at you!" (This seemed questionable given my tone and volume.)

"I am mad at this stupid computer!" (But so far yelling at it hasn't been helpful.)

"I feel like I get stuck all the time, and then I can't get my work done." (Code for: I believe my work is more important than yours.)

"I hate computers. They are from the devil." (Absurd hyperbole to try to get a reaction.)

This was an actual conversation.

My husband paused on the phone. It was a really long pause. It was so long I held out the phone to look at my screen to see if we were still connected. And then he said, "It's hard for me to help you when you are angry. And I can't really help you right now because I need to be in front of your computer, and I have to get to a meeting. I can try later tonight. I have to go. I love you."

And that was it.

I hung up the phone and felt a jolt in my soul. I needed that truth. *We* needed that truth.

This cycle of me being a victim of my circumstances and expecting my husband to rescue me was no longer working. That's because it just wasn't a true narrative. I was not power-less. I had options. I could solve my own problems. I could look up videos to see what the problem was. I could take a walk and regain composure. I could breathe. I could do a different task and come back to this problem. I could call my friend who likes to solve computer problems and said he would be happy to help anytime. I could choose joy even when the rains came, the flood rose, the wind beat against my emotional house. I could take responsibility.

Accepting responsibility is a humbling thing. Confessing our issues, our problems, our weaknesses leaves us feeling quite vulnerable. But the light always shines through the cracks. Letting the truth be the truth is freeing. Putting down blame opens up our hands to accept responsibility. It gives us the space to choose to own what we can, and that will help us to be whole.

Later that night I apologized to my husband for the cycle of blame I had helped create. I apologized for being mad at him when he had zero responsibility for my computer problem. I told him I was sorry for thinking I needed to be problem free to be happy and for how often that affected our marriage. We laughed. We cried. We started a new cycle (one in which I decided my husband would be my last and final resort when it came to technology). As imperfect as it has been since, it has been better. We are going for just a little bit better, one day at a time.

Accepting responsibility and the practice of solving my own problems has been one of the most refreshing gifts to our relationship we've had in a long time. And I imagine it will pump fresh air into your relationships too. May we be people who accept responsibility, who confess our weaknesses, and who stop blaming others and start owning our own lives. May we know we have a great deal of power right inside of us.

A Practice

The spiritual practice of confession banks on the forgiveness and healing of Jesus. Forgiveness has happened because of the Cross, and we can be restored into right fellowship with Him any time we sin. Scripture tells us, "If we confess our sins, he is faithful and just and will forgive us our sins and purify us from all unrighteousness" (1 John 1:9, NIV). This is our private moment with God to come humbly and to name our weaknesses and sins, asking Him for forgiveness.

This week, practice confession. Ask God for forgiveness for what He brings to mind. Then practice confession to those you have hurt. Your spouse? Your roommate? Your children? Your coworker? Who do you need to confess to and ask forgiveness from?

A Prayer

As you breathe, let this prayer flow from you.

Exhale: God, I confess my dependence upon myself.
Inhale: I receive Your forgiveness, and I depend on You.

11

TAKING OFF THE TRAINING WHEELS

Starved for Becoming

I clearly remember the day we took the training wheels off of my son's bright red Lightning McQueen bike. We lived on Main Street, a four-lane road with trucks going by constantly. Life on that very busy street meant my son would be learning to ride a bike on the side streets and alleyways next to and behind our house.

My son wanted to take off his training wheels. And also, he didn't. He was both nervous and brave; he wanted to ride without those wheels, but he didn't want to feel the pain and the scrapes that could come from a fall. He held it all in his heart: the fear and the fun, the joy and the jitters. But it was time, and we all knew it. So, we took them off. And as it turned out, the learning was just as much for us as it was for him. I had to learn to let go; he had to learn to go on his own.

I noticed right away that if he tried to look back at me, he would swerve, wobble, and fall. He needed to learn to look forward, to see the road for himself, to anticipate the bumps and cracks on his own, to think for himself, to focus on the road in front of him. He knew I was there behind him, cheering him on. But I couldn't pedal for him; this was his to do. I could clap for him, and shout out suggestions, and be present, but this was his time to learn, grow, and become a bike rider on his own.

There is a lot of learning when it comes to riding a bike. There is a time to have training wheels and a time to get the next best bike for your skill level. There are bumps and bruises, there are near misses and collisions. There are scary downhill moments and hard-to-climb uphill streets. But if anyone is to become an experienced bike rider, they must keep learning and navigating and growing. They must experience new terrain, venture onto new paths, and engage with communities who have new ideas on how to ride, stay hydrated, change a tire, or build endurance.

Riding a bike—and living our lives—is a growth curve of becoming, not a destination of arriving.

WE ARE BECOMERS

Believing we have arrived in any part of our life keeps us stagnant and stale. It starves us of the opportunity of becoming. The belief that there is nothing left to learn—that we've arrived or figured it out or cannot change our minds—can keep us from embracing the beautiful gift of growth that can nourish us. Being open to changing, learning, and becoming is part of our design. With Jesus, there is always a chance to become something new—someone new.

In Matthew, we find one of the hallmark calls to follow Jesus:

> Come to me, all you who are weary and burdened, and I will give you rest. Take my yoke upon you and learn from me, for I am gentle and humble in heart, and you will find rest for your souls. For my yoke is easy and my burden is light.
>
> MATTHEW 11:28-30, NIV

Learning, growing, changing, unlearning, deconstructing, breaking—this is what it means to follow Jesus. He challenged the political, social, and spiritual structures and systems. He crossed lines, borders, and norms. He flipped tables and changed minds. He brought healing. He was teaching a new way of life—a new way of becoming. Part of learning from Jesus means we stay pliable and moldable, like clay in the hands of a good potter. We learn from Him, we trust Him, we follow Him, and we become more of who He made us to be each step of the way.

We are not called to have every theological stance figured out and cemented down. Instead, we are simply called to keep in step with the alive and active Spirit who leads us, guides us, transforms us, and moves us. The moment we believe we have arrived—having fully developed views, thinking patterns, and behaviors that cannot change—is the moment we have left behind the fulfilling adventure of becoming.

Later, we read more on this way of learning and becoming from Paul. In his letter to the Romans, Paul writes, "Do not conform to the pattern of this world, but be transformed by the renewing of your mind" (Romans 12:2, NIV).

This renewing of the mind? It's a becoming. It means we are learners, we are doubters, we are question-askers, we are seekers, we are apprentices on the job. The more we give ourselves over to renewing our mind, the more our thoughts, our lives, our actions, and our whole sense of being will change for the better. The more we'll become like our Teacher.

After all, this is part of God's design. We were made to become. We are becomers.

KEEP GOING

Here's the truth friend: this journey of becoming isn't easy. Learning from our Teacher, renewing our minds, continuing to grow into the people God made us to be? This stuff isn't going to happen overnight. Just like my son needed to be reminded that he was capable, safe, and brave while learning to ride his bike, we need the constant reminder that God is in the work of helping us become. God is in the details of our becoming. The good, the hard, the long, the difficult, the celebratory—God is right there cheering us on and encouraging us to keep going.

> God is in the details of our becoming.

Recently, I was asked to preach a sermon at a fantastic church in Toledo that has become so dear to me. I had gotten to know their women leaders and spoken at their events. They love Jesus, they love each other, and they love their city. I was delighted to be back, ready to leave a trail of encouragement behind me.

That morning, I found myself praying that if there was a woman in the back, in the dark, who had maybe come on her own, that she would feel like God's beloved in a way she hadn't in a long time. It was such a specific prayer—an image I had when I was praying for their congregation. I hardly ever get images like this, and if I do, I hardly ever follow it with praying for that image. But this time, I did. I just couldn't shake the idea that God wanted to use me to speak to that woman, who-ever she might be. So I prayed for her—this nameless, faceless woman in the back row—just before I stepped up to speak.

As I wrapped up my message and the worship band began to play, the hosts that morning decided to give away a few copies of one of my books. And friend, guess who received a copy? A young woman sitting in the back of the room, in the dark, by herself. A young woman I had envisioned that morning. A young woman God put on my heart to encour-age. It was a new experience for me to have a faint vision of someone in need, to pray for her, and then to see God answer that prayer. My hope is that this woman walked away feeling encouraged by God in a new way that morning, because I know I certainly did!

I walked through the parking lot to my taupe minivan with a sense of joy and satisfaction at a job well done. That sermon? I had written and taught it on my own, listening to the Spirit-Helper inside of me. Almost every other sermon I had taught up to that point had relied heavily on the voices around me, almost more than the Spirit of God Himself. But this time, I listened to the Lord. I let God lead me not just in preparing the message but in delivering it. And God kept me going, each step of the way, making good on His promise to use me for His glory and, in this case, for the good of a woman in the back row.

As I left the parking lot, my van a quiet sanctuary, I felt a deep sense of the Lord speaking to me.

Amy, I have given you everything you need. You can do this; you just did this. You taught and blessed people. You trusted me to use you to encourage others. Trust my Spirit-Helper. You are becoming more of who I made you to be each time you choose to keep trusting, keep trying, and keep going.

It was clear to me that morning that I was still becoming. I was stepping into more of who God had made me to be, honing the gifts I have been given, listening to the Spirit's leading in my prayer life, and following wherever He would take me. They were small steps, yes, but they were steps on the journey of becoming. And they were steps that encouraged me to keep going.

Sometimes I think we've forgotten who we are. That we are called to keep going, keep growing, keep changing, keep learning, keep becoming. To not get spiritually stale. To not let our souls get stuck like that one uncle you see every Christmas who has the same glasses and flannel shirt he's had on for two decades. We are called to become. We are called to keep going.

And when we choose to keep moving toward the person God made us to be, we can trust that He will nourish, care for, and satisfy us each step of the way.

This brings to mind something we are called by the prophet Isaiah: "So they will be called oaks of righteousness, the planting of the Lord, that He may be glorified" (Isaiah 61:3, NASB).

We are mighty trees that grow taller, more mature each year. With deep and wide roots, we may bend, but we don't break through the terrible storms of life. We sway and clap and sing about God's beauty. We shed old leaves and grow new buds each year. We become fuller, brighter, more beautiful. We keep going and keep growing until we've developed into the mighty oak we were born to be.

We are oaks of righteousness—people who grow and become more like the good and gracious Gardener who planted us for His glory.

BREAKING TO BECOME

Have you ever watched a baby chick come out of her shell? Me neither. But YouTube has, and watching it there I discovered that it's hard work! A tiny fledgling of a chick pecks away at her protective shell, bit by bit, eventually breaking the egg that has kept her safe. It's a brutal end for the shell that's been her home for so long, but it's a necessary step in the process of becoming. Sure, she could stay in her shell and never become anything else. But there, she would starve. This breaking is the only way she can come out, grow, and eventually fly.

There is no becoming without breaking. Breaking is part of becoming. Some ideas need to be broken down. Some wings need to be broken through shells. Some lies need to be broken in half. Becoming comes from breaking.

> There is no becoming without breaking.

For years, I was afraid to break the shell surrounding me. The ideas felt too sacred. My questions felt too doubtful. The structures felt immovable. Maybe you feel some of the same right now. Friend, we cannot be afraid to break in order to find beauty! So I think it's time to start pushing on the shells that surround us so we can break free and become more like the God who made us.

Where do you feel yourself cracking open the shell around you as you follow Jesus? What are you slowly but surely breaking free from?

Legalism?

Patriarchy?

Sexism?

Purity culture?

Christian nationalism?

Systemic racism?

The abuse of power?

Fear?

Perfectionism?

What questions are you asking that may crack the shell around those things? Be encouraged, friend! Questioning the status quo was Jesus' jam. Because questions break structures. Curiosity breaks systems. Wondering breaks rigidity.

Let yourself crack the shell and see who you become outside of it.

After all, isn't this the kind of breaking Jesus modeled for us? Jesus broke the rules on the Sabbath. Jesus broke the unspoken systems of racism and sexism. Jesus broke the rule that a woman's testimony was not valid. Jesus broke preconceived ideas of what it means to know God. Jesus broke social norms by having prostitutes at His table and cheaters over for dinner. Jesus broke well-oiled legalism. Jesus broke old ways of thinking and gave new thoughts. Jesus often said, "You've heard it said . . ." and then followed it with, "But I tell you . . ." It's part of the model of breaking to become. Jesus broke so much in order to build His Kingdom. That's because breaking down is necessary for building up.

The more I have studied and considered how Jesus operated, the more I have noticed so many things breaking down in order for something beautiful to emerge. For me, the most prominent breaking to become is in regard to women. Seeing the way Jesus broke the societal norms in the way women were treated and valued and seen in the culture and the church broke something in me. Or rather, I broke free from a theological shell built around me as a female in the church—a shell that was starving me from fully being able to become in that space.

Truth be told, I've always felt second class when it comes to leadership in the church as a woman. What about female leadership all the way from top to bottom? What about female pastors and elders? What did this look like under Jesus' leadership? When I look at Jesus' words and actions on the subject, this is what I see:

Jesus revealed that He was the Messiah to a woman first.

Women joined His flock.

Women learned and traveled with Him.

In a society where a woman's place was in the kitchen, Jesus encouraged women to cross the line and learn from Him.

The very first commission to go share His resurrection was to a woman—a woman (whose testimony wasn't considered valid in court) was the first one to give the Good News.

After Jesus' resurrection, the Holy Spirit gave gifts to women and men alike—gifts that are nongendered.

Both men and women taught.

House churches were held and supported by women.

As the church began, we watched the redemption of the equality in co-reigning (as set up in the Garden) take place after the defeat of the grave.

I love how Imago Dei Community in Portland, Oregon, puts it: "In the Gospels, we see Jesus setting the people of God on a new course concerning the roles of men and women. In His treatment of women, Jesus planted the seeds of change that grew into a fuller expression and outworking in the life and ministry of the early church."[1]

Feeling like I couldn't step into the calling God had on my life simply because of my gender? It was starving me. But breaking out of my little, tiny, confining shell, poking my wings all the way out, and flying? That's where I've found real satisfaction.

Even as I write this, I know this idea of women leading in every possible way in the church is a difficult one for some. And honestly, I could be wrong on some of this. I am quite open to being wrong; it's part of the process of becoming. But I'm writing it down anyway to share that sometimes, little crack by little crack, we are allowed to explore, to shift, to question, and to change our minds. We are allowed to learn new thoughts and wonder if there's an angle we are not seeing. We are allowed to grow for God's glory. We are allowed to explore, to question, and to flip a table or two. As Jesus taught us, we are allowed to break as we become.

IN THE GRAY

I'll have you know more and more has become gray to me in my faith, leaving a very few solid things black and white, steadfast and true. The chief black-and-white truth that I can stand on still is this: Jesus walked this earth, was crucified, was buried, and rose three days later. He is King, and His Kingdom reigns. This is an outlandish miracle that I base my whole life upon. This is a truth I can stand on in my becoming.

Almost anything else in Christianity? Really smart people on all sides have built theological cases to back up their thoughts. So, I will keep learning, I will keep growing, I will keep developing into a mighty oak—planted and cultivated by God Himself. I will keep trying to hear His voice and keep in step with His Spirit-Helper. I will keep breaking and becoming, even in the gray.

Friend, don't miss my point here. I'm not suggesting we walk away from the parts of faith that are messy, or hard, or difficult. I'm not suggesting we choose what serves us and leave the rest. There's starvation in that line of thinking too.

What I am suggesting is we lean into the places that feel gray. We ask questions, we take them before the Lord, we look for what's true and real and honest in those spaces. I'm suggesting that instead of turning away from the gray, we turn toward it in order to make sense of it.

For me, the biggest shift I've seen in this movement toward the gray has been in regard to how I see my body.

First, my body. What a wonder, you guys! Many of us have been told that we, as women, are the problem. More specifically, our bodies are the problem. Our thin spaghetti straps are thick with temptation. Our curves are too dangerous. Our wet hair reminds men that we were naked in the shower, so we should dry it before being in public. (Yes, this was an actual statement from an actual man said to my actual ears one summer on a mission project.) Our skirts are too short. Our thighs are too lovely. When it comes to purity, our bodies have been labeled as the enemy.

It's all been entirely too convenient that this belief system on the female body has come primarily from men. They told it to us, and then, we as women started telling it to each other too. I have certainly been part of the retelling of it all. I thought it was black and white, but as I've grown—as I've become—I realize now that it's just not. And I am so very sorry.

I was learning and growing inside of purity culture, and I had no idea. Purity culture took its seat on the throne, dictating how women ought to be seen, how they ought to feel about their bodies, how they ought to bend for men in every way. And in that culture, women started starving.

Can I just remind us what God said about us when He knelt down in the dirt and created human beings from the dust? As He breathed life into our precious bodies, He spoke a blessing over us—something categorically different from the rest of creation.

He called us *very* good.

In the first five days, God created light, sky, water, vegetation, stars, and creatures. And the repeated phrase is, "and God saw that it was good" (Genesis 1). But when He created human beings, a shift occurred. God stopped what He was doing, turned His face toward us, gazed at our amazing and beautiful physical bodies that He had just handcrafted in His own image, and called us *very* good: "So God created mankind in his own image, in the image of God he created them; male and female he created them . . . *God saw all that he had made, and it was very good*" (Genesis 1:27, 31, NIV, emphasis added).

From the mouth of God Himself, our bodies are very good. They are made in God's very own image and likeness—a reflection of Him. We are made by Him, made for Him, and made like Him. And because of that, we are very good. When I found myself starving under the weight of purity culture's message about my body, I came back to this truth for nourishment.

I am *very* good. My body is *very* good. When I embrace that truth over anything else, I am free to become more of the person—the woman—God created me to be.

I want to say a blessing over you, friend, about your body: God made you, and God loves what He made. Your body is not evil or bad or a problem. Your body is amazing and stunning and precious. Your body can hold babies, hug humans, reset broken legs, perform amazing brain surgery, create gorgeous music, and knead delicious sourdough. Your body can sew intricate quilts, make amazing love, lead meetings, create office cultures, dig well, sweat out toxins, and garden gorgeous plots of dirt. Your body can sing, dance, cry, love, breathe, and laugh. Your body is a masterpiece made by the most creative and brilliant Master. You are a created whole person—body, soul, mind—all integrated inside of skin.

And it is all *very* good.

My hope is that when you read that last part, you're filled up with freedom, love, and joy. That the places where you are starving to see yourself as a very good creation would feel just a little bit more nourished, a little bit more fed, a little bit more comforted. That you find space to break free from the black and white and move toward the gray. That you find permission to become.

BELIEVE TO BECOME

Along the way, I have also grown when it comes to using my gifts. After one of the first Sundays I preached at my church, a sweet older woman came up to me and said, "You have a gift. Thank you. You are anointed to teach." I was taken aback by this bold statement and kept it close to my chest for a while. Did she have some kind of inside knowledge? No one had said that before to me: anointed. But then, more voices over time joined hers in telling me God used me to speak to them when I taught. Others said they were seeing things in a way that they hadn't seen before. And eventually, I started to believe that God had given me a gift. And from that belief, I started to become. Once I believed I was capable of filling the call God had given me in my own life, I was able to step into it fully. I was able to become more of who God made me to be.

In a conversation author and scholar Heather Thompson Day had with author and ministry leader Karen Swallow Prior, two profound things were said in regard to our gifts and our calling.[2] Day said that when you want to know where you are going, look behind you. In other words, past affirmation can be a path to your future. Prior responded that the very nature of calling—literally being called by someone—is that it comes from the outside. My takeaway is this: if we are to keep growing and becoming, we need to be both people who encourage others in their gifts and people who take the encouragement from others to keep using the gifts we have.

But what if you don't know what your gift is? What if you think you have a gift to give but don't know how to best use it? What is your gift for? Let me encourage you, friend: every single person has at least one spiritual gift given from our Creator. And He gave us these gifts to encourage and edify the body of Christ. When we recognize and use those gifts, we're not only making a way for ourselves to become more of who God called us to be, we're helping the entire body of Christ do the same. Look at how Paul put it:

Just as each of us has one body with many members, and these members do not all have the same function, so in Christ we, though many, form one body, and each member belongs to all the others. We have different gifts, according to the grace given to each of us. If your gift is prophesying, then prophesy in accordance with your faith; if it is serving, then serve; if it is teaching, then teach; if it is to encourage, then give encouragement; if it is giving, then give generously; if it is to lead, do it diligently; if it is to show mercy, do it cheerfully.

ROMANS 12:4-8, NIV

We are called to growth and maturity. We are called to use our gifts to grow the body of Christ. And in order to do that, we have to believe. We have to believe that we are called. We have to believe we are able. We have to believe so we can become.

As tenderly planted acorns that grow into oaks, we are called to keep becoming. We have the freedom to shift, to change, to fail, to learn, to discover, to explore, to try, and to try again. Do not let the need to have everything figured out stifle the becoming inside of you. Don't let the fear of failure keep you from trying to become. Don't let the pain of breaking stop you from becoming. And don't let there be a day you don't believe that with God you can become.

May we give ourselves permission to stay pliable and moldable, to keep growing and becoming.

A Practice

Congrats! By reading this book, you are practicing the spiritual discipline of learning! You are processing information, focusing on God's Word, and taking in new thoughts and ideas about nourishing your soul. I am proud of you.

Now, keep going! Think of one way you can continue learning, growing, and becoming in Christ this week. Look at your schedule and carve out time to be a learner, a grower, a becomer. Where do you need to grow in your spiritual understanding? Who could you learn from or what can you read to continue to become?

A Prayer

Remember, becoming is a journey, not a destination. So as you work toward becoming, step by step, use this prayer for God's guidance, encouragement, and wisdom.

Father, I need Your help to become the person You've made me to be. I need Your voice to lead me in becoming. I need Your wisdom to guide my steps. I need Your discernment to break the beliefs and ideas holding me back. I need Your encouragement to believe in the gifts You've given me and my ability to use them. I can't become without You, Father. So as I continue to grow, learn, and become, continue to walk with me, each step of the way.

12

THE POWER OF YOUR PEOPLE

Starved for Community

I remember the year the switch flipped inside of me.

My husband and I had been married for four years, enjoying our quaint little married life (with no money, of course). The blue town house we lived in was within walking distance of our college downtown. We were real adults with real jobs living in a real adult residence. I was working full-time on staff with the college ministry Cru, and my husband was working as a graphic designer in downtown Toledo. Once a week we led a life group with Cru for college students in our little town house just off campus. Other nights, we would play disc golf, taking time to play all eighteen holes. Sometimes we'd have friends over for dinner or have time to ourselves to just chill. Our time was our own; our life was our own. We had leaned right in and cozied up to life on dual incomes with no kids.

Until the switch flipped—the "I want a baby switch." It was as if I had gone to bed one evening content in my situation, and while I was sleeping, the Motherhood Mice snuck into my bedroom, ran up the bedposts, and turned on the motherhood switch in my brain. The proverbial biological clock began ticking on me. What had previously been "Meh" was now a full-out "Yes!"

I was ready to have a baby.

And so we tried to get pregnant. A few months went by. Then a few more months went by. Eventually, a year went by. Each subsequent period felt like a funeral for my hopes and dreams. A funeral for what could have been but hadn't made it into reality. A funeral for the yearning inside of me that hadn't come to life—as indicated by the blood that showed up instead of the baby.

Eighteen months went by. Then twenty-four months. Still nothing. Instead of holding a baby, I held frustration, anxiety, grief. I held hopelessness. I held jealousy. I held comparison. I held judgment. I held pain.

Finally, in our twenty-fifth month of trying, we found out we were pregnant. We were shocked, amazed, and thrilled. Our firstborn son made it into the world six weeks early, welcomed by loving aunts, uncles, grandmas, and the nurses who cared for him for twenty-three days in the NICU. Life with a little boy was sweet and funny and hard and silly. It was everything.

When my son was about three, the switch flipped again. We both wanted him to have a sibling. So we tried to get pregnant.

A few months went by. Then a few more months. This time, twenty-seven months passed, and there was still no baby.

I was beginning to despair . . . again. That's a lot of months hoping, praying, and crying.

Months that left me sad, low, and depressed. During Sunday mornings at church—especially during worship—the tears would just fall. I would grieve and sing, sway and cry. It was therapy, and it was vulnerable, and it was tender.

A COMMUNITY OF PEOPLE

My husband has been our worship leader for two decades now. During those years of infertility, he would often sit down next to me after worship and put his arm around me and my tearstained shirt. One particular morning, I leaned over to him and said, "I think we should ask the elders in our church to pray for us that we get pregnant."

He looked at me, nodding his head slowly. "Do you mean . . . today?"

"Yes."

"Okay . . ."

I knew what was running through his head. Maybe I knew it because I was thinking the same thing.

That's a pretty humbling thing. You want us to go to some of the older men in our church and have them pray that we get pregnant? That feels like a really intimate request.

Whether or not he was actually thinking that—even if it was just me who thought it—I didn't care anymore. I was at the end of myself and my competency and my abilities, and

I felt like God was reminding us that we were given a community of people—a family—with whom we could share our hurts, our burdens, and our lives.

When our pastor ended the service, my attentive husband pulled the elders of our church aside. We all stepped out the side door of the sanctuary into a secluded hallway. These men, one by one, surrounded us. These were men who had walked by faith. Who had seen their own grown children endure hardships, divorce, infertility, job loss. Who had experienced their own failure and grace, grief and disease. They had known God to be good on the mountain and in the valley. These men didn't bat an eye about praying for a baby. This was part of walking by faith with their community.

I will never forget the day that we found out we were pregnant with my sweet girl, Olive. I looked at that pregnancy test and ran to find the calendar. I knew all kinds of things about when I was ovulating and when we were trying. When I realized the date of our conception, I was shocked. It was that day we were prayed for—the day these men, by faith, asked that a baby be knit together inside me. My sweet baby girl who just turned ten is a product of the faithful prayers from our community of people.

Friend, let me just stop here to acknowledge that this story may be sensitive for you. Because I know that there are so many women whose faithful prayers for their family have remained seemingly unanswered. I know there are many who have walked a road through infertility much longer than I did. I know that there are women who've had a community of people figuratively putting hands on their bellies to pray for God to expand their family.

If this is your story, I want to say this: I am praying. I am praying over your pain. I am praying over your body. I am praying over your family. I am praying for your womb to be filled, for your heart to be cared for, for your trust in the Lord to stand firm no matter the outcome. The power in a community of people surrounding you is valuable beyond measure. You may be starving for someone to walk alongside you right now, the way these men did for us. Friend, please find nourishment in knowing that I am part of the faithful community of people who are praying for God to move in this area of your life.

CREATED FOR COMMUNITY

Here's what I believe to be true for all of us: God does not want us to go it alone. He created us for community. He created us to crave the presence of others. He created us to carry each other's loads together. He created us for family life, where He is our good Father and we are surrounded by brothers and sisters. He created us to find nourishment by gathering with others. He created us to forgo isolation to taste the gift of community. And our biggest proof? God Himself is a built-in community, His own party. Father, Son, Spirit—all one. This is such a divine mystery and a consecrated community. And as we are created in His image, so we were created for community.

> As we are created in His image, so we were created for community.

That cold January day at church, I didn't want the whole congregation gathered around us. I wanted a few trusted people who had walked through pits and darkness around us. I wanted the presence of people who were safe to share our burdens with. I wanted the loving arms of people who would come around us without shame or judgment.

I wanted community because that's what God created us for.

If I hadn't been open to God's leading to share with our community that day, we would have missed out on the gift of having their support. We would've missed out on the chance to be encouraged by their prayers. We would've remained starving in our isolation instead of nourished by the community God designed for us.

Maybe you know the feeling of isolation too. Whether it's the result of a move to a new neighborhood, illness, a change in life stage, or simply a struggle to step out and find your people, you know full well the ache that comes from isolation. In that space, we aren't working as well as we could be. We aren't being loved and cared for or loving and caring for others as we are called to do. We are starving, missing the good gift of God's community.

We are missing out on a piece of what we were created to crave.

ENCOURAGEMENT IN GATHERING

Being isolated from community breeds a lot of things, one of the most dangerous being apathy. Eventually, we begin to believe we don't need other people. We stop trying as hard to meet with other people. We give up on gathering because we simply don't think it's that big of a deal.

Friend, that apathy is starving us. It's cutting us off from finding the gifts that come in gathering with God's people. It's cutting us off from the encouragement that can be found there.

The chief reason stated in Hebrews for regularly gathering as a people set apart to follow Jesus? To encourage one another. When we are cut off from the community of believers, we are cut off from giving and receiving encouragement.

The beauty of encouragement is that it literally means to infuse courage into someone. Anyone need courage to keep going? To trust God? To believe that today matters? To deny yourself, take up your cross, and follow Jesus? To choose to serve instead of being served? To be last and not first? To stay connected to the Vine, the source of our joy? To live differently than our culture?

Yes, I know I do.

What a good and gracious God we have that He would be so very mindful and compassionate toward us as to build in encouragement as one of the chief benefits of gathering. This is what Hebrews says:

> Let us hold tightly without wavering to the hope we affirm, for God can be trusted to keep his promise. Let us think of ways to motivate one another to acts of love and good works. And let us not neglect our meeting together, as some people do, but encourage one another, especially now that the day of his return is drawing near.
>
> HEBREWS 10:23-25, NLT

Just this week at church, one of the dearest older women in our congregation came over to me in tears. She lost her husband about a year ago and has been walking the painful road of grief. Many of us have been walking with her through this loss. Glassy eyed and timid, she asked to speak with me. Lightly touching my arm, she said, "Thank you. Thank you for what you wrote in your post a few days ago. You said we are not stuck. We can grow, learn, and change. I needed that so much. Stuck is the word that has been in my mind over and over. And when I read that, I felt a deep sense of freedom. I felt unstuck. Thank you." I was overcome by her kind words, and then we hugged. Later that day she messaged me that this moment was everything. She had wanted to quit. She had not wanted to get out of bed. She had not wanted to come to church. But she did. And being in community, in close proximity, was a lifeline for her that day. It was a lifeline for me, too. I needed her hug, her connection, her maternal care. The blessing was mutual. Both our lives were richer for our connection.

This was a holy moment of courage infusion. It was the gift of encouragement that can only come from connecting to other believers in community. It could only have happened in a space where we could walk over, face to face, and share the gifts of encouragement and affection with each other.

We both left that moment a little bit taller, a little bit stronger, a little bit lighter, and a little bit freer. Because we had gathered, and had shared courage. Because we had linked arms, shared tears, and spurred one another on.

We run the risk of missing out on this good and holy

encouragement when we let apathy tell us we don't need it. When that happens, we fall out of the practice of gathering, and eventually, we start starving for the goodness of encouragement. For the goodness of being known, loved, and cared for by others. For the richness and strength from those who have battled and overcome, who have a limp to prove the battle was costly but worth it. For the joy of having spiritual aunts and uncles, moms and dads, brothers and sisters who can love and encourage us like only a spiritual family can.

I don't want to miss out on the good that God has for me in community. I don't want you to either! May we all find nourishment for our starving spirits in the presence of other believers.

THE BODY OF CHRIST

After all, this shows God created us to function together: a body of believers!

Paul writes on this at length in his letter to the church in Corinth:

> The human body has many parts, but the many parts make up one whole body. So it is with the body of Christ. . . . So God has put the body together such that extra honor and care are given to those parts that have less dignity. This makes for harmony among the members, so that all the members care for each other. If one part suffers, all the parts suffer with it, and if one

part is honored, all the parts are glad. All of you together
are Christ's body, and each of you is a part of it.

1 CORINTHIANS 12:12, 24-27, NLT

The day we got pregnant again, we were reminded how
we are all a part of something much bigger than ourselves.
Isolation keeps us small and disconnected, but community
reminds us we are so much stronger and better together. And
being a part of a body is where the magical beauty of it all
comes in.

Being a part of the body—whether eye or hand or foot
or stomach—keeps us dependent on the rest of the body to
work well. We have a proper place, a proper design, a proper
position in the body because God has put each part where He
wants it. And being a part of the body keeps us humble. No
matter how significant, prominent, shiny, earthy, or pedes-
trian we appear. No matter whether we use a microphone or a
spreadsheet or a forklift. No matter our gender, race, or socio-
economic status. We are welcomed into the body simply by
believing in and following God with our lives. It is all only
because we are integrated and connected to the greater body.

When we called the elders who had laid hands on us to
share our joy in this new life to come, it was a gift. They were
with us in our starvation and despair, and now they could be
with us in the nourishing and flourishing. We all cried tears
of joy, hugged, and enjoyed mutual affection as my belly grew
and our faith strengthened. We were in it together, a body of
believers each doing their part.

God has put each one of us just where He wants us for

the body. He made us, He designed us in light of the whole entire body, and He placed us carefully in that body. The gifts you have been given were given to you on purpose. They're by design for you and for the body as a whole. The moment you start wishing to be a different part of the body ought to be a signal to you that something is off. The Snake is telling you lies about who you are and where your value is. When comparison creeps in about how you help the body of Christ to function, remember that is not from God.

> God has handpicked how He wants you to fit into the body.

An eye gets to help the body in a different way than a hand, but they experience each other and need each other, and they are integrated in community with one another. God has handpicked how He wants you to fit into the body. He is masterful at good design. He knows what works best for the body, and you are a part of that grand and beautiful design.

We need your gift. We need your ability. We need you to function. We need each other. If we stop showing up, stop coming together, stop gathering? The body would be missing something beautiful and vital. It would be missing *us*.

A RISK WORTH TAKING

Of course, we all know how risky it is to gather together regularly. It's not all roses all the time, is it? The same body we come to for encouragement has also most likely hurt us at some point. We may have to take the time to heal from the hurt that comes from the very body that is supposed to give us life. Please find healing, dear one, if you have been hurt by the body. Trust me, that pursuit of healing is a worthy use of your time. If we choose to live in accountable friendships and have deep relationships, we are bound to be hurt by one another. This is part of fumbling forward in a broken world. But the good news is, there's always more to the story with God. In His community, we are also bound to be blessed by one another in beautiful ways. Flawed, messy, imperfect people sharing their lives is a risk, but I have to tell you that it is absolutely worth it.

You know the cartoon guys that step on a two-by-four and it flies up and smacks them in the face? Their foot caused the pain to their head. It hurts, so much so that they see little birdies circling their head when they hit the ground. But immediately after the board hits their head, their hand comes to the rescue. The hand holds the ice, bringing comfort and stability.

Our body of believers functions the same way. When we are hurt by the body, other parts of the body can bring healing. If one part of the body injures another, a different body part comes to rescue and heal. So it is with community. We get to give and receive grace, catch each other as we stumble, heal the wounded parts, encourage and enjoy each other as we go.

We get to take a risk worth taking.

There's a story of a village where the women came to the river daily to wash clothes and linens. When the washing machine was introduced, slowly each home got their own machine. Of course, this saved time and was quite efficient. But then, something else entered the homes of these women.

Depression.

They couldn't figure it out. What happened? What changed? Why?

The washing machine.

The women lost their daily routine of companionship. They weren't sharing each other's loads (laundry and otherwise). They were cut off from the lifeblood of community and connection.

Community is not always efficient, but we weren't created to be efficient. We aren't human doings; we are human *beings*. That means, we're created to *be* together. We're created for community, for connection, for caring for one another. We're created to find nourishment in the presence of others.

Here's to the practice of living life together, in the God-given gift of community.

A Practice

If you have been out of the practice of gathering, ask yourself why. What keeps you from gathering? What is keeping you isolated? What could be some of the side effects of falling out of the rhythm of gathering together?

This week, consider what it would look like for you to move toward community again. Make a plan to gather with other believers this week as a first step!

A Prayer

As you breathe, let this prayer flow from you.

Inhale: I am a vital body part.

Exhale: I am created for connection and community.

13

WELCOME TO MY PITY PARTY

Starved to Give Thanks

"Where are you?"

"On a park bench where I belong," I responded pathetically.

My husband paused, unsure of the next best course of action.

"What do you mean? You're on a park bench? What do you mean 'where you belong'? I just got home from work, and you're not here. I was worried about you. What is going on?"

"I can't get a job. I try all day long. You get to work, and be useful, and use your degree, and be productive. What am I even doing with my life? I have nothing to show for it. I feel worthless. I'm just going to live on this park bench."

We had been married for one month. What a bride.

The very word for what I was feeling in that moment is descriptive: self-pity. "Pit" is built right into it, and that's exactly where I felt I was that day. On a park bench in a deep, dark inward pit of self-focus and self-loathing. The actual definition of self-pity isn't much better than the way it feels: "a self-indulgent dwelling on one's own sorrows or misfortunes."[1]

If I had a dime for every time I indulged in my own sorrows, we could all vacation in Fiji. But sadly, no one has ever issued me a cent for my pity parties. Self-pity never pays off. It leaves us nothing more than alone on a park bench at the end of the day.

And I know because I've wallowed in my fair share of it over the years.

Like the five-year stretch of motherhood when my babies were little and we were in the weeds of diapers and wood blocks and naps and sippy cups and Cheerios and laundry and spit-up and baby food—and I was bitter because I felt stuck. I felt small and unseen. I felt frustrated. I felt stunted in my hopes and dreams of writing and speaking. I wanted to be out THERE, but I was stuck in HERE with these children who would cry if I set them down. Children who needed me constantly and who couldn't have adult conversations and who made every day feel like the same day.

Welcome to my pity party.

For a long time, I let myself stay in the pit of despair and self-pity. I looked at everyone else's lives and idolized their circumstances, jobs, marriages, and ministries. I looked at myself and saw failure and worthlessness at being "just a mom." I belittled the significance of my work and glorified the significance of the work of everyone else. And you know what? It made me miserable.

There in the pit of self-pity, I was starving.

WHY ME?

Self-pity can be the root of a lot of destruction and depression. But what is the difference between sadness and self-pity? Where is the line of allowing space for mourning dreams and unmet expectations and for naming the hard things? One clue for me to know if I'm indulging in self-pity is this phrase entering my mind on repeat: *"Why me?"*

These two little words say so much. The first is a cry for purpose and meaning. We think if we have the answer, it will satisfy how we feel and relieve our thirst for justice. But even when we are given an answer, it hardly cures the feeling.

When cancer hit my beloved grandma and she passed when I was in high school, we didn't know much for sure about why it happened. The only conclusion we could come to was that we live in a broken, fallen world, and cancer is part of the brokenness. Does that answer help? Not really. It's still incredibly frustrating, sad, and awful. It doesn't change the outcome either. She still passed and left us all feeling robbed of so much. Knowing anything about why wouldn't have changed that.

The "me" of the question is where self-indulgence comes in. It's where I move into the center of the universe. What can begin as grief or sadness can easily slip into self-indulgence. It's what leads me to the false belief that I am the only one who

> **Self-pity makes our world very small and dark and leaves us starving for something better.**

has ever suffered or known pain or experienced loss or been rejected. Self-pity makes our world very small and dark. And of course, it leaves us starving for something better.

We aren't the only ones to cry out "Why me?" in our moments of pain and despair. We aren't alone in our tendency toward self-pity. Besides the fact that so many wise psychologists tell us this is very common to humanity, we also join a whole host of biblical characters who sat in the "Why Me?" mud themselves. Let's take just one for example: Jonah.

Jonah was commissioned by God to bring conviction over sin, and ultimately the good news of mercy and compassion, to the wayward city of Nineveh. Jonah didn't think they deserved it, and honestly, he was right. Not one of us deserves the grace God gives us to be forgiven, to be set free from condemnation, and to know God. Grace means undeserving favor, and the people of Nineveh felt so very undeserving to Jonah.

So Jonah put himself on the judge's bench to decide what was just and what was not. He didn't think offering grace to this terrible city was right, so he ran from the task of delivering it. I think you guys know what happened next, right? Jonah was eaten by a big fish. But God, in His mercy and grace, didn't leave Jonah in the belly of the whale for long. He had the fish spit Jonah up just in time to try again. Sometimes the grace of a stinky huge fish can be so sweet.

After three days in the gut of a whale, Jonah finally went to Nineveh and shared about God's grace, and the whole city—all 120,000 people—repented! Talk about a revival. How amazing!

But Jonah?

He was still mad and miserable. He was still frustrated by God's mercy for Nineveh. These people didn't deserve God's compassion. It wasn't right, and Jonah didn't like being the one to deliver it. So, he sat under a plant to sulk, really still hoping the Ninevites might get smitten after all. But then God sent a worm to eat the plant, and Jonah was left with no shade. Now, he was angry all the more.

It seemed Jonah found more joy in the plant that gave *him* shade than in the compassion God gave *to a whole city*. Jonah wanted to be right, and he wasn't. He wanted his way, and he didn't get it. He imagined this was a path to joy, and all it produced was misery. It was all about him and what he wanted, not about God and His desire.

Welcome to Jonah's pity party, friend.

In response to what's going on in Jonah's heart in that moment, God says something important to him:

You pity the plant, for which you did not labor, nor did you make it grow, which came into being in a night and perished in a night. And should not I pity Nineveh, that great city, in which there are more than 120,000 persons who do not know their right hand from their left, and also much cattle?

JONAH 4:10-11

From the moment God sent Jonah to Nineveh, Jonah was asking the question, "Why me?" And the result? A self-indulgence in his own sorrows that hardly let him thrive. He was starving from the start. The moment he thought he knew better than God, his life became a miserable mess. But what I love about the way God handles Jonah here is that he does so with the same compassion and grace offered to the people of Nineveh. If Jonah had pity for a measly plant, shouldn't God have more than that for His people gone astray?

Jonah almost missed this truth because he thought he knew better than God. And friend, don't we do the same thing all the time? How often do we focus on the small plants that have withered in our lives? How quickly do we allow self-pity to take root in us, so much so that we don't see the beautiful forest of grace shading us all the while?

CHIN UP

Just yesterday I forgot to set a timer for a new special dessert I was making for my son. I realized this much too late when I smelled burnt honey coming from the oven. As I flopped the charred pan on the stove, I said for all to hear, "I hate my life."

My husband ever so kindly said, "Huh! That's what our son said earlier this morning when his leg hurt."

Gut punch received.

My little seven-year-old was echoing his momma. He hated his little life because his momma hated her life. I love exaggeration, hyperbole, and over-the-top drama. It's just funny to me! But I had no idea I was actually modeling self-pity to my kids, and they had bought it, hook, line, and sinker. This is not who I want to be or how I want to raise my kids. I didn't want them to starve the way I was starving in my own wallowing.

I had to get out of the pit. Maybe you need to do the same.

So, how do we do it? How do we climb out of the pit of self-pity?

Well, we can start by listening to the words of my amazing father who always said, "Chin up, baby doll." In other words, if we want to get out of the starving pit of self-pity, we have to look up. We have to lift our chins up and shift our perspective from ourselves to our God. We are often just one perspective shift away from gratitude. From moving away from pity and toward peace. From being thankful, whether in the pit or out of it.

So start with that chin up, friend!

Of course, I know this is no easy task. Sometimes our starving souls make it difficult to even find the strength to lift our heads. But friend, we must try. Because when practiced enough, this new perspective comes easier. And eventually, it becomes a beautiful way to live. A way to feed our starving souls with the nourishment of gratitude.

I want to make an important distinction here. Lifting our chins up doesn't mean we ignore the muck around us. My dad was brilliant at acknowledging the pain. Before he would affectionately say, "Chin up," he would examine the hurt and assess the problem. He would make space for tears, woes, and all manner of sadness. He would see me where I was before helping me lift my eyes somewhere greater.

I remember playing softball when I was about nine years old. My dad was the assistant coach, always cracking jokes with us, always encouraging us, always helping us step to the ball when we swung, and always telling us to keep our elbows up for a level swing. During one practice, I was running for third, and the next thing I knew, I was a mess of gravel and gloves. My knee stung, and so did my pride. I limped to the bench and cried my eyes out.

My coach-dad came jogging over, sat right down next to me, and told me what a great run I'd had. He couldn't believe his eyes when I stole that base and went for third! My tears kept falling, but less so as he told me how fun I was to watch. He commented on how much of a scare I gave my teammates because I was coming in so fast. He casually asked if he could see my skinned-up knee. Pulling a raggedy old tissue from his pocket (the quintessential dad move), he wet it and dabbed my knee. He then took his trusty red and white water jug that seemed older than me and poured more water on my knee, washing the gravel down my leg. I winced, but the tears subsided.

He saw the pain and the scrape. He let me be sad. He told me how great I was. He dressed my wound. And then he sat there with me for a while, telling me jokes, watching the practice next to me, checking on his daughter—his beloved.

And then he said, "Chin up, baby doll. I think you could probably get back in there. Your team needs you. What do ya think?" And so, I lifted my head and looked out at the field. My teammates were getting into their positions. Third base was wide open, waiting for me. My friends were waving me in. I looked up at my dad, hugged him, and slowly walked back out to the field with my chin up.

Self-pity keeps us navel gazing. It keeps us missing the world around us. We miss all of its beauty, all of its glory, all of its goodness, all that God is orchestrating, creating, and building. But when we lift our chin up, we can see the loveliness out there. We can see the wonderful people we are invited to enjoy. We can see all of the things we are invited to do. When we stop focusing on ourselves and choose to look to our good Father cheering us on, we can climb out of the pit and can get back into the game.

It's a choice, this perspective shifting. But we have a good God who specializes in helping us do this. Take great comfort as the Psalmist says: "But you, O LORD, are a shield about me, my glory, and *the lifter of my head*" (Psalm 3:3, emphasis added).

It seems my dad tore a page right from the Father's playbook. He listens to our tears, heals our wounds, and then tells us, "Chin up, daughter. Look at Me. Look at all that's around you. There's so much here for you to enjoy. Really see it. And then get to it."

THE PRACTICE OF GRATITUDE

If we want to stop feasting on our self-pity, then we must practice gratitude. It's one of the easiest ways to lift our heads. It's one of the best ways to find nourishment for our souls. Self-pity focuses on ourselves and what we think we deserve. So often, I am starving because I'm focusing on what I do not have. Or, I believe that what I do have ought to be better. But the real, actual truth is this: we always have God. Self-pity may tempt us to believe otherwise, but the reality is God is always with us and available to us. And because of that, we always have a reason to be grateful. When we focus on God, gratitude will flow, and those waters will raise us up out of the pit. Because God is more than enough in absolutely every moment of our life.

His grace is enough, perfected in our weakest place.

His love is enough, bringing security when everything is shifting under our feet.

His forgiveness is enough, giving us freedom from the need to punish ourselves or wallow in self-defeat.

His provision is enough, equipping us with shelter, food, and strength.

Truly considering that God is good—that He is enough—will nourish our souls and lift us out of the pit of self-pity.

An article in *Psychology Today* says that gratitude is one of the keys to combating self-pity.

> It's hard to feel self-pity and gratitude at the same time. Self-pity is about thinking, "I deserve better." Gratitude is about thinking, "I have more than I need." Mentally strong people recognize all that they have to be grateful for in life—right down to the fresh air to breathe and clean water to drink.[2]

The day I burned that dessert, instead of saying, "I hate my life," I could have chosen to say something like, "Well that was frustrating. Good thing we have enough ingredients to make it again." I could have told the truth of the sting I felt in seeing the time and energy I spent on the dessert go to waste. And I could have also seen the gift of abundance in front of me—enough for another dessert.

The practice of gratitude can come in all shapes and sizes, but the key is to practice. When we make a habit of gratitude, we'll see self-pity become easier to resist. And eventually, we'll see it turn to peace.

> When we make a habit of gratitude, self-pity becomes easier to resist.

THREE WAYS TO PRACTICE GRATITUDE

To help us get started on this practice together, I want to share three simple ways we can find gratitude in our daily lives.

The first is *paying attention to your senses*. This looks like taking a breath and using your five senses to stay present in your current reality. It allows you to stop worrying about the past or being anxious about the future, and instead, to really see what is right in front of you. For me, one of the best ways to practice this is to get outside and observe nature, thanking God for the gorgeous blue sky, the funny little birds, the sound of the leaves in the breeze, and any other detail that moves me that day. I find my blood pressure lowers and my body releases tension when I use my senses to practice gratitude.

The second is *keeping a gratitude journal*. This is an intentional practice of writing down at least five things you're grateful for each day. Try to be specific with each gift you notice. If you are thankful for your job, what specific part of your job are you grateful for? I have a friend who started this practice by keeping a gratitude journal on the Notes app in her phone. Eventually, she read that the physical act of writing is extremely beneficial to remembering (forgetfulness is one reason why we aren't grateful), so she now carries a very small notepad in her purse to record what she is thankful for throughout the day. I like to start the morning by journaling about five things I'm grateful for. It puts my mind on gratitude before my feet even hit the floor.

Finally, *sharing your gratitude with others* is a way to say out loud the gifts you see. This encourages whoever you are telling, and it helps you actually notice and name the goodness around you. Over time, you are using your mouth to breathe life around you and to lift others out of their self-pity pits. You are giving your gratitude to someone else, nourishing them with your words. And who knows? That may be the beginning of a life-changing shift in perspective for them, too.

And the benefits of gratitude are amazing. The experts tell us gratitude is pretty life-changing! It boosts our mental health, it helps us accept change, and it can relieve stress. When we practice finding the beauty and training our eye to see the lovely, we can accept the change when we are thrown curveballs in life. Because we can find the gift even in the change. We can see the grace even in the pit. We can discover beauty even in the ashes.

Be encouraged, dear one. You don't have to stay starving in the pit of self-pity. You can begin to lift yourself out with the nourishment found in gratitude. It's not difficult; it just takes practice. May we be people who leave our pits of self-pity with our chins up, thankful for all that's around us.

A Practice

From the Old Testament to the New, the Bible is full of the call to thanksgiving. Take time this week to find a few verses that speak to the practice of gratitude and thanksgiving. As you read those passages, think about how you can choose this week to practice gratitude in your own life. And as you practice, remember the words of my friend Barb Roose: "For now is not forever." Whatever you are facing that may take you deep down into the pit of self-pity, it is for now, not forever. Seasons change. God is present. And beauty is still all around us. Chin up, dear one.

A Prayer

As you breathe, let this prayer flow from you.

Inhale: God is the lifter of my head.

Exhale: I can be grateful for the gifts God has given me each day.

14
EVEN IF . . .
Starved to Fast

I sat in front of my word processor trying to concentrate long enough to write a paragraph. Even a morsel of a sentence would do. Just a crumb of a concept would be helpful. But my thoughts wouldn't budge. My words wouldn't come out to play.

I was distracted by the growling of my stomach and the waning of my energy.

I looked around at the beige walls in the bedroom of my college apartment which were strung with photos and decorated with a few pieces from my art classes. From the crack in the not-quite-sealed windows, a subtle draft hit me again, so I grabbed a blanket and wrapped it around my shoulders.

I tried to write again, but the hunger pangs called. I grabbed the spoon and the bowl of cold water sitting beside my books. I slurped the water from the bowl like it was cereal or soup or stew. I was eating my water like it was food because I felt desperate.

I was starving.

My friend and I were on the second day of a three-day fast. I kept thinking about what my mentor had said about the spiritual discipline of fasting: *"Fasting without prayer is starvation."* Nothing felt truer in my small, cold college apartment at that moment.

I felt like I was the worst faster who had ever fasted. I had tried praying, but I felt hungry, and angry about being hungry, and a little bit sick because I was so hungry, and angry that I felt sick from being so hungry. You get the picture. Fasting proved to be one of the most humbling practices I had ever tried, and it left me feeling mostly angry. Not at all holy, or enlightened, or closer to God, or really better in any way. With each passing hour and each pang of hunger, I just felt worse. This was not going well.

I had fasted a few lunches before this full-on, three-day fast. In those times, instead of eating lunch, I spent the time on a prayer walk—a walk that mostly consisted of chattering to Jesus and looking forward to dinner. As I prayed, donuts danced in my head, warm plates of lasagna floated by in my mind, hot buttered biscuits swirled around me. I wasn't supposed to be thinking about food; I was supposed to be thinking about God. I wasn't really killing the fasting game then, either.

GRABBY HANDS

Friend, as it turns out, fasting is hard. And the reality is, it may not work the same way for everyone. Some may be called to fast full meals for days at a time. Others may be called to fast from practices or habits or things that distract or tempt us on a regular basis. The point isn't necessarily what we fast; it's why we fast.

Nothing reduces us to our primal instincts like being threatened with hunger. All manner of grumbling, complaining, dissention, stealing, and greed come out. We get grabby with hands and hearts. In short, we are hangry in just about every way.

I think that's because fasting is a discipline that reveals what controls us. And so often, we would rather not find out! Of course we have our guesses, but we don't want to actually experience our hands being pried from those things, do we? We don't want to let them go. But friend, it seems if we want to nourish our souls, open hands might be a huge part of that nourishment.

If we go back to the Garden, so much control was at play with that gorgeous piece of fruit. Yes, it was about the fruit, but it was also about the things the fruit represented: control, power, and knowledge. It was the allure of being like God. It was the appeal of taking matters into our own hands. It was the belief that we could feed our own souls.

Look at it again:

When the woman saw that the fruit of the tree
was good for food and pleasing to the eye, and also

desirable for gaining wisdom, she took some and ate it. She also gave some to her husband, who was with her, and he ate it. Then the eyes of both of them were opened, and they realized they were naked.

GENESIS 3:6-7, NIV

The fruit was beautiful to the eye and desirable for gaining wisdom. And so Adam and Eve's grabby hands took hold of the fruit in hopes of taking hold of the things it promised. But we know how this story goes, don't we? Grabbing for that fruit did the exact opposite. It cut them off from the nourishing supply of life—from the only One who has it, our Creator-King. All in one bite, they were starving.

FAST TO FEAST

Friend, starvation in any form isn't what God wants for us. That's why, when Jesus fasted, He pointed us right back to the One who feeds us.

Right after Jesus was publicly affirmed by His Father at His baptism, the Spirit of God led Him out to the wilderness. And there, He fasted . . . for forty whole days! The devil slithered over to Jesus, tempting Him to make His own bread by turning stones to scones. Could Jesus have done it? Absolutely! But He knew that bread wasn't the answer. It would feed Him physically, but it wouldn't nourish Him spiritually. Instead, Jesus reminded Himself, reminded the devil, and reminded us that we don't live on bread alone.

What do we feast on instead?

"On every word that comes from the mouth of God" (Matthew 4:4, NIV).

God has always been our sustainer. He sustains us by providing our breath, our shelter, our food, our water—everything we need in this life. I love how author Richard Foster puts it: "In experiences of fasting we are not so much abstaining from food as we are feasting on the word of God. Fasting is feasting!"[1]

Fasting is actually feasting, friend. Fasting is so much more than just the removal of something; it's the replacing of something. We must replace what's starving us with a feast—a feast upon the things of God.

And feasting on God's Word is a great place to start! As Jesus fasted in the desert, every single response to the devil was from God's Word. He countered every temptation with Scripture. He feasted on the goodness and sustaining nature of the Law, the Prophets, the Psalms, the historical books, and more. He feasted on God's Word, and it sustained Him in the face of famine.

> **Fasting is so much more than just the removal of something; it's the replacing of something.**

THE WHY

Looking to Jesus to understand the feast in our fast? It helps us get to the why behind fasting: to worship, experience, and know God. Fasting is all about communing with God at His abundant table of grace, mercy, and compassion. Over and over again, God says fasting is to bring us closer to Himself.

To crave Him.

To hunger for Him.

To thirst for Him.

This is why it's so important to check our hearts when we choose to fast. If we're going in with the wrong motives, we'll walk away feeling little more than starved. The prophet Isaiah spoke at length about this, warning the Israelites that if their fasting was actually just false humility or an attempt to earn the praise of others, they would find no reward. God, through Isaiah, eventually confronts the Israelites, who had been fasting and were still wondering why God had not answered their prayers. God's response to their frustrations peels back the layers to reveal their true motives:

> "We have fasted before you!" they say.
>   "Why aren't you impressed?
> We have been very hard on ourselves,
>   and you don't even notice it!"
> "I will tell you why!" I respond.
>   "It's because you are fasting to please yourselves.
> Even while you fast,
>   you keep oppressing your workers.
> What good is fasting
>   when you keep on fighting and quarreling?
> This kind of fasting
>   will never get you anywhere with me."
> ISAIAH 58:3-4, NLT

The Israelites were using God. They were using Him, through practices like fasting, to get what they wanted. But as they fasted, they continued to live unchanged lives. They treated their workers poorly, oppressed others, didn't give generously to those in need.

And God saw right through it.

Fasting with entitlement is like throwing filthy rags down at God's feet. He doesn't want it. But fasting with humility? This is where we find God. This is where He will guide us continually, give us water when we are dry, restore our strength. This is how we become like "a well-watered garden" or "an ever-flowing spring" (Isaiah 58:11, NLT). It's such a beautiful promise, isn't it? When we fast with true humility, we will feast in the presence of God.

> When we fast with true humility, we will feast in the presence of God.

Later, Jesus also points right at the motive behind fasting.

When you fast, don't make it obvious, as the hypocrites do, for they try to look miserable and disheveled so people will admire them for their fasting. I tell you the truth, that is the only reward they will ever get. But when you fast, comb your hair and wash your face. Then no one will notice that you are fasting, except your Father, who knows what you do in private. And your Father, who sees everything, will reward you.

MATTHEW 6:16-18, NLT

If the why behind our fasting is for others to think highly of us, our fasting won't serve much purpose. That's why Jesus goes so far as to instruct us to fast in private. To not make it about anyone other than ourselves and God. There, in our quiet humility, we will find the reward.

SEEK FIRST

Praise be to God, we don't have to do it alone! Through His Spirit, Jesus will most certainly join us in our fast. All it takes to invite Him to the table is a small start.

A mustard seed of humility.

A kernel of confession.

A tiny bit of repentance.

In the same way that a small amount of yeast works its way into an entire loaf of bread, Jesus is always willing to work with small things to create big change. He isn't asking too much. He's asking for just a little bit. We can start right where we are. Confess what comes to mind. Repent for what He reveals. We can bow our head slightly and see what bounty comes to us there.

The key at the end of Jesus' discourse is this: "Seek the Kingdom of God above all else, and live righteously, and he will give you everything you need" (Matthew 6:33, NLT).

Seek first—or look first at God—as you fast.

Even when your heart turns toward food to satiate you, turn your attention back to God to sustain you.

Even when your hand reaches for your phone to distract you, look back at God for discipline to put it down again.

Even when you're tempted to make a purchase you know you don't need, seek God to help satisfy you in other ways.

When you're struggling to stay the course in fasting, turn your attention back to God and His goodness. Look back at God one hundred times if you need to. And every time you do, do so without shame! This is about coming to the One who offers bread without cost as often as you can. The more you turn to Him, the better! I promise He will meet you in this. He will sustain you. He will bring refreshment.

All you have to do to begin is seek.

Since my ambitious three-day fast in college, I have taken a much less aggressive route to this practice—a route that starts small and focuses on seeking first. I have fasted with a small group for a half day once a week for the course of a month. I have fasted for breakfast and lunch, breaking my fast at dinner. I have fasted from certain kinds of foods. I have fasted to hear Him. I have fasted when at a crossroads. I have fasted to know which way to go.

Of course, I have never done it perfectly, but perfection is never the point. Fixing our eyes on the author and perfecter of our faith (see Hebrews 12:2) and coming humbly with empty stomachs to be filled with God's Word—that's the point.

Each time I have fasted, I've done so clinging to God and His Word like food and water. And each time, He has led me, guided me, and revealed to me the next step. It has been so good and so hard to feast on the character of God and to trust Him just a little bit more than when I started the fast. But to experience being filled with peace in the middle of the longing to be filled? To find that I can survive on the Word and it is good and nourishing? To know I can be nourished by God alone?

That's worth the work of seeking, fasting, confessing, repenting. It's worth it all!

EVEN IF

Friend, I think it's important to note that, as with any spiritual practice, there's no magic formula. We can come humbly, plead prayerfully, and fast with pure hearts to seek God first, and still, we can walk away without the outcome we wanted.

Years ago, my dear friend Erik was dying of cancer. He was on staff in the same ministry I was, and his wife was one of my best friends. We adored Erik—his humor, his silly antics, his heart for the Lord. We loved him and did not want to lose him on this earth. So, we fasted and prayed for God to save him. We pleaded with God to heal the cancer in his brain. We asked God to have mercy on him and his family.

And Erik died.

My tears tasted so bitter when we got the call. I'm writing with tears in my eyes just remembering that season. Erik left behind two young sons and a wife. He left behind a community of people who loved Jesus and had prayed on their knees for his healing. We fasted, and he died.

Why, Lord?

Fourteen years later, I still have no answers. But what I do have is this: the assurance of God's presence and promises found in Scripture.

There's one passage I feasted on during those days that I will never forget. It has since shaped my faith, my life, and the dark times that came after Erik's passing and beyond. When I first sat with this Scripture during those difficult moments, I wasn't sure I could say it. I wasn't sure I could claim it with conviction. But now, I know I can.

When three men in the book of Daniel—Shadrach, Meshach, and Abednego—were thrown into the burning furnace because they would not bow down to King Nebuchadnezzar, they said something that spoke of their great faith:

> If it be so, our God whom we serve is able to rescue
> us from the furnace of blazing fire; and He will rescue
> us from your hand, O king. But *even if* He does not,
> let it be known to you, O king, that we are not going
> to serve your gods nor worship the golden statue that
> you have set up.
>
> DANIEL 3:17-18, NASB (EMPHASIS ADDED)

Even if He does not.

I was driving to Indianapolis to stay with Erik's wife, crying and worshipping God and praying and fasting over this very verse.

Even if He does not.

I was asking God for a miracle. For help. For time. For anything.

Even if He does not.

I was begging God to save the father of these two young

boys. I was pleading that they would grow up in his presence and experience what a good man he was.

Even if He does not.

God did not save Erik.

And then, I was left with a choice. We all had a choice. Would we still serve God, who is able but chose not to do what we fasted and prayed for?

Yes.

Even if it's painful.

Even if we're disappointed and devastated.

Even if the outcome isn't what we hoped for.

Even if we don't understand.

I say yes.

And I keep saying yes. I said yes when we walked through infertility. I said yes when anxiety and depression arrived. I said yes when Crohn's disease showed up. And I will keep saying yes because Jesus said yes for me—for all of us—on the Cross.

Even if He does not do what every ounce of my being is crying out for, I still will not serve another god. I will trust the good King. I will trust that His ways are far above any of my ways. I will trust that He is good when I don't see any good.

This truth has become bread to me in the deserts. It fed me when I had nothing else to eat. It kept me from starving in despair.

Though He didn't rescue Erik from the fire, God still walked in it with him. He walked with all of us, too.

He never left us.

He never abandoned us.

He never turned His back on us.

He was there. He is there. He will always be there. And that is the goodness of the King that I will bow down to even if.

A REASON TO FAST

Friend, I believe we all have a reason to fast.

And I wonder, what does God have to say to you? What does He want to speak to you? What does He want to settle for you? What does He want you to know about His character? What might you need to take with you from His Word? What does God have for you that may only be found by the putting down of something in fasting and the picking up of the feast of His Word?

When Erik was dying, this brought us to fasting. This was our reason. But throughout the course of our lives, we'll find different reasons to fast. In fact, we find different reasons for different fasts all throughout the Bible.

- Esther called a fast for safety when faced with death. And she saved both herself and her people. (Esther 4:16)
- Nehemiah fasted in grief when he learned Jerusalem's walls were broken down, leaving God's people vulnerable. And God helped them rebuild the wall. (Nehemiah 1:1-4)
- Ezra declared a fast for deliverance as he and the returning exiles traveled. And God provided. (Ezra 8:21-23)

- Jonah saw Nineveh repent, and fasting and prayer was part of their repentance. And God saved them. (Jonah 3:10)
- Judges records a corporate fast for victory over the Benjamites. And God gave it to them. (Judges 20:26)
- Jesus prepared for ministry through fasting in the desert and came back into the synagogues with the power of the Spirit. (Luke 4)
- Anna worshiped God through fasting and prayer. She was eighty-four and waited for decades for the coming Messiah. (Luke 2:37)

What I love about each of these instances and so many more in the Bible is that the reason for fasting was never a command. It was always about the practice of seeking God, trusting God, depending on God. It was about the heart. And when a heart is weary, overwhelmed, afraid, grieving, fearful—this is when we see the men and women of old fast to center on God, the giver of life and nourishment.

So consider your reason to fast right now. And friend, do so with a heart to draw near to God. May it not be a heavy burden for you to take on, but rather, a path and a practice to knowing God.

The God who doesn't leave us to starve.

The God who created us and knows exactly what will feed our starving souls.

The God who has good things in store for us.

The God who has compassion and joy, even in—especially in—the face of sorrow and hardship.

The God who nourishes us.

A Practice

This week choose one way to practice fasting. If you are able, fast for a meal or even for a day. Or fast from a habit or practice, like social media, television, shopping, or your phone. Consider what Scripture you plan to also feast upon. (Hint: Psalm 103:1-5 is a great place to start!) You might want to journal, pray, or meditate on the Scripture as you fast and draw near to God.

A Prayer

As you breathe, let this prayer flow from you.
Inhale: I hunger for You, God.
Exhale: I am satisfied in You. You are the Bread of Life.

EPILOGUE

My son was diagnosed with Crohn's disease in 2018.

That's when everything changed.

It resulted in quite a lifestyle upheaval for our whole family. We had to throw out everything we knew about food and embrace a new way of eating. Because the old way wasn't going to nourish him anymore. Sure, he could've been stuffed with food, but his condition left him starving. In order to truly nourish him, we had to forsake the old kingdom in our kitchen for a new one.

And friend, it was really, really hard.

There were no cheat days or fudging here and there. With this new diet, something was either allowed or completely off limits. It had to be if we wanted to heal his gut, calm his inflammation, and put his body back into remission. If we didn't want him to starve, we had to start over by feeding him with the things designed to help and heal.

So, that's what we did.

And by day three, my son was pain-free.

This diet began to change his life, but that change didn't come without cost. It was a massive shift in our rhythms, our ingredients, our budget, and our taste buds. But in the end, it's been worth it. Because now he's satisfied, he's nourished, he's healthy.

Now, he isn't starving.

The same, I hope, is true of you.

Friend, we've seen our own spiritual starvation. We've acknowledged it up close. We've addressed what might be cutting us off from the real source of life and nourishment in Christ. We've navigated what it looks like to start being fed by the only One who can satiate us.

Now, it's time to make the change.

We can't simply stop here. We've got to change our spiritual diets. We've got to implement the practices and prayers that will feed us. Just like my family had to change the way we thought about food and what we did with it, we as believers have to change the way we approach spiritual nourishment in order to truly be fed.

> **We have to change the way we approach spiritual nourishment in order to truly be fed.**

So, let's keep the pantry sweep going. Keep tossing the things that are threatening your overall spiritual health. Keep cutting out the stuff that only pretends to nourish. Keep replacing the old with the new for the sake of your soul. Keep going, friend! Because small changes over time make a great impact, both here on Earth now and in the Kingdom of God we long for.

Friend, know that I have prayed over these pages. That they would be a gift and a blessing and a revelation. That you would realize you have the power, through God's Spirit, to believe new narratives and practice new spiritual rhythms. And that from believing who God is and practicing being in His presence, you would find nourishment.

May we find that God truly does "give us this day our daily bread."

Let's not overlook the importance of the words here: give us *this day* our daily bread.

We must keep a daily dependence on Him for today's nourishment. We're not called to store up something from God for later, but instead, we're called to believe in His presence, today. To be nourished by His truth, today. To receive the daily bread that will satisfy us, today.

He wants to be with you, today.

He wants to restore you, today.

He wants to nourish you, today.

May we choose to step out of starvation and into the nourishing, satiating, fully satisfying ways of God.

Here's to food only the Father can give.

Amy

APPENDIX

Action Steps toward Justice

- Join Be the Bridge at bethebridge.com. This an online community of authentic, racial bridge-builders. Their About Us page states, "Our vision is that people and organizations are aware and responding to the racial brokenness and systemic injustice in our world. That we are no longer conditioned by a racialized society but are grounded in truth. That all are equipped to flourish."[1]

- Commit to working through the online material in Be the Bridge. You can start here: bethebridge. com/get-started/.

- Listen to podcasts to educate yourself. Here are some ideas to get started:

  - *Code Switch* (an NPR podcast about race and identity)
  - *Still Processing* (hosted by two culture writers for the *New York Times*)

- *Nice White Parents* (serial *New York Times* productions about building better school systems)
- *1619* (a *New York Times* production)
- *Be the Bridge* (about cultivating conversations that lead to real change)
- *Tent Talks* (a podcast focused on renewing the social and political imagination)

- Start following Black, indigenous, Latinx, Asian, and Pacific Islander voices on social media. Start to intentionally see, hear, and listen to people of color in your social media feeds.
- Find local organizations that fight for justice and equity so you can learn from them and show support through your time, talent, and treasure.
- Commit to reading one antiracist or indigenous author's book per season this year. Here are some books you might consider (Note that these authors come from a variety of faith backgrounds. Even if their worldview or values differ from yours in some areas, there are things we can learn from each of them.):

  - *Be the Bridge* by Latasha Morrison
  - *Human(Kind)* by Ashlee Eiland
  - *The Color of Compromise* by Jemar Tisby
  - *White Awake* by Daniel Hill
  - *I'm Still Here* by Austin Channing Brown
  - *First Nations Version: An Indigenous Translation of the New Testament*

- *Divided by Faith* by Michael O. Emerson
- *Reading While Black* by Esau McCaulley
- *Jesus and the Disinherited* by Howard Thurman
- *The Cross and the Lynching Tree* by James H. Cone
- *Rescuing the Gospel from the Cowboys* by Richard Twiss
- *Living in Color* by Randy Woodley
- *One Church, Many Tribes* by Richard Twiss

ACKNOWLEDGMENTS

What you are holding is a compilation of the teaching and influence of so many. I sit here grateful for the privilege of being able to print my words. So thank you, dear reader, for picking up this book and for allowing God's Spirit to do what He wants to do in you. I pray you will continue to allow Him to lead you from starvation to true satisfaction in Him.

I want to acknowledge my friend and copilot over twenty years of ministry, Steve Rieske. Your words, ideas, and influence are all over these pages. You have forever shaped how I see the world with a gospel lens, and you continue to push me to carry a cross instead of a sword. I am very much like our old brother Peter—prone to swift sword use. And to my dearest friend, his wife, Sandy. I'm grateful for all the walks and talks and shared ministry. You are a gift and a constant source of support and encouragement.

I want to acknowledge my friend, educator, and bridge builder Martha Chandran-Dickerson for asking hard questions, sharing vulnerable moments, holding my hand through justice work, and understanding the good, hard, raw process of protecting the imago Dei in each one of us. I guard the imago Dei in you, sister.

To Greg Dickerson, Toni King, and Crystal Martin, who have sat at my table, by my fire, in my home, and at restaurants together and shared honestly about what it's like to navigate this world as Black brothers and sisters. Thank you for your leadership in my church and in our community. You bring light and life wherever you go.

To my acquisitions editor and chief encourager, Kara Leonino. You took me on and believed in me. You have been nothing but a tall glass of encouragement and have held a hard-core belief in my gifts. I am so grateful to call you a friend and to be cared for and coached by you. You are a joy to me, and I am beyond grateful to work with you!

To the Tyndale Publishing team. Sara and Stephanie, your edits were lifesaving. Truly. Kristen, you are such a gift in getting this message out there. To Jen and your designs—this was an obvious choice. I'm in love with this cover. Thank you.

To the community groups I have been a part of at Brookside Church for twenty years. So many of you have taught me so much, including how to grieve, how to laugh, how to love, how to have a puppy and lead a Bible study at the same time, how to serve, how to celebrate, how to eat good food, how to be aunts and uncles to one another's children, how to hug, how to drop off meals, how to give candy to children, how to heal. You have nourished my soul. To Erin, Sara, Jamie, and a Marco Polo channel that won't quit and is full of tears, laughter, stories, and recipes. To Suzy and the year we were self-proclaimed coworkers. To Trinity and the summer days, the ski trips, the talking over everything. To Lori, the easiest friend in all the world.

To my parents, who said I could do whatever I put my heart into. And here I am. Thank you for your constant metaphorical and actual cheering in every part of my life. To my sister, who would light anyone's car on fire who double-crossed me and whose laughter goes unmatched in my life. If we are starved for anything, it might be to laugh until we are on the ground. And that is where you constantly deliver.

To my three children, Robby, Olive, and Judah-bear. Thank you for letting me tell your stories, your battles, your weaknesses. I have seen God lead our family to green pastures, and I count on the Shepherd to do so in your individual lives. You are my joy and my crown. If nothing else, listen for His good voice. He loves having you close.

To my husband. This is where I run out of words. Do I thank you for twenty-two years of all the disc golf and tennis and playing and laughing and late-night conversation and good food that began in college and continues to this day? Do I marvel at the goodness of God in whispering to me, *That one* when I first saw you? Do I count the ways you have let me cry, walk away, and fight with you about the deepest scars I carry? Do I share how you lead me out of starvation and toward Jesus' table of grace, mercy, righteousness, and justice all the time? I'll just say this: you are my forever love, and I am beside myself at your constant tears of pride and joy for me.

NOTES

CHAPTER 1: PHONE-A-HOLICS UNITE

1. Trevor Wheelwright, "2022 Cell Phone Usage Statistics: How Obsessed Are We?" Reviews.org, January 24, 2022, https://www.reviews.org/mobile/cell-phone-addiction/.
2. Russell Moore, *Tempted and Tried: Temptation and the Triumph of Christ* (Wheaton, IL: Crossway, 2011), 20–21.
3. James Bryan Smith, *The Good and Beautiful God: Falling in Love with the God Jesus Knows* (Downers Grove, IL: InterVarsity, 2009), 168.

CHAPTER 2: CHANGING THE SOUNDTRACK

1. Brené Brown, "Listening to Shame," filmed March 2012 in Long Beach, CA, TED video, 13:55, https://www.ted.com/talks/brene_brown_listening_to_shame?language=en.
2. Brené Brown, "The Power of Vulnerability," filmed June 2010 in Houston, TX, TED video, 12:33, https://www.ted.com/talks/brene_brown_the_power_of_vulnerability/transcript.

CHAPTER 3: HUMBLE PIE, ANYONE?

1. Rick Warren, *The Purpose Driven Life: What on Earth Am I Here For?* (Grand Rapids, MI: Zondervan, 2013), 262.
2. Sue Bohlin, "Isn't It Egotistical of God to Command Our Worship and Praise?," Probe for Answers, Probe Ministries, September 3, 2009, https://probe.org/isnt-it-egotistical-of-god-to-command-our-worship-and-praise/.
3. C. J. Mahaney, *Humility: True Greatness* (Colorado Springs, CO: Multnomah, 2005), 65–70.
4. Tim Keller, *Gospel in Life Podcast*, episode 541.

CHAPTER 4: PRAYING POLITICS

1. Zachary Wagner, "Jesus Is Not a Republican and Christianity Is Not Nationalism," Center for Pastor Theologians, January 11, 2021, https://www.pastortheologians.com/articles/2021/1/11/jesus-is-not-a-republican-and-christianity-is-not-nationalism.

CHAPTER 5: IMAGO DEI

1. Matt Stieb, "Amy Cooper Didn't Learn Much from Her Time as 'Central Park Karen,'" Intelligencer, New York, May 26, 2021, https://nymag.com/intelligencer/2021/05/amy-cooper-didnt-learn-much-from-being-central-park-karen.html.
2. Rochelle Olson, "Legal Analysts Say Emotional Eyewitnesses Amplified Powerful Video as Witness to Chauvin's Crimes," Star Tribune, April 20, 2021, https://www.startribune.com/legal-analysts-say-emotional-eyewitnesses.-amplified-powerful-video-as-witness-to-chauvin-s-crimes/600048315/
3. "George Floyd: What Happened in the Final Moments of His Life," BBC News, July 16, 2020, https://www.bbc.com/news/world-us-canada-52861726.
4. Amber Tucker, "4 Lessons on Anti-Racism from Brené Brown and Ibram X. Kendi," Mindful, June 19, 2020, https://www.mindful.org/4-lessons-on-anti-racism-from-brene-brown-and-ibram-x-kendi/.
5. "The Middle Passage, 1749: A Spotlight on a Primary Source by Robert Livingston," History Resources, Gilder Lehrman Institute of American History, accessed April 3, 2022, https://www.gilderlehrman.org/history-resources/spotlight-primary-source/middle-passage-1749.
6. "Racial Justice," Equal Justice Initiative, https://eji.org/racial-justice/.
7. Tim Keller, Justice and Generosity (New York, NY: Penguin, 2010), 2–3.
8. Keller, Justice and Generosity, 10.
9. Brenda Richardson, "Redlining's Legacy of Inequality: Low Homeownership Rates, Less Equity for Black Households," Forbes, June 11, 2020, https://www.forbes.com/sites/brendarichardson/2020/06/11/redlinings-legacy-of-inequality-low-homeownership-rates-less-equity-for-black-households/amp/.
10. Richardson, "Redlining's Legacy."
11. Rebecca Nagle, "Invisibility Is the Modern Form of Racism against Native Americans," TeenVogue, Condé Nast, October 23, 2018, https://www.teenvogue.com/story/racism-against-native-americans.
12. Bernice A. King, quoted in Verse & Voice "Voice of the Day," Sojourners, December 14, 2021, https://sojo.net/daily-wisdom/verse-and-voice-12142021.

13. Latasha Morrison, *Be the Bridge: Pursuing God's Heart for Racial Reconciliation* (Colorado Springs, CO: Waterbrook, 2019), 23.
14. Morrison, *Be the Bridge*, 7–8.
15. Morrison, *Be the Bridge*, 8.
16. Morrison, *Be the Bridge*, 39, 41.
17. Adam Weber, "4 Best Steps toward Healing Racism from a Conversation with Latasha Morrison," Crosswalk, July 30, 2020, https://www.crosswalk .com/special-coverage/racism/best-steps-toward-healing-racism-from-a -conversation-with-latasha-morrison.html.
18. Morrison, *Be the Bridge*, 154.

CHAPTER 6: REST IS ON THE WAY
1. Marva J. Dawn, *Keeping the Sabbath Wholly: Ceasing, Resting, Embracing, Feasting* (Grand Rapids, MI: Eerdmans, 1989), 19.
2. Eugene Peterson, *Working the Angles: The Shape of Pastoral Integrity* (Grand Rapids, MI: Eerdmans, 1989), 73.

CHAPTER 7: A PLATE FULL OF ANXIETY
1. Kaitlin Curtice, "How to 'Try Softer': A Conversation with Aundi Kolber," Sojourners, February 19, 2020, https://sojo.net/articles/how-try-softer -conversation-aundi-kolber.
2. Sarah Tuckett, "Calming 4-7-8 Breath," Sarah Tuckett blog, April 13, 2020, https://sarahtuckett.com.au/calming-4-7-8-breath/.

CHAPTER 8: ALL BY MYSELF
1. Tim Keller Sermons Podcast 538.

CHAPTER 10: PLAYING THE BLAME GAME
1. Gregory L. Jantz with Ann McMurray, *Controlling Your Anger before It Controls You: A Guide for Women* (Grand Rapids, MI: Revell, 2013).
2. Paul David Tripp, "Why Did Water Come Out of the Bottle?," YouTube, July 31, 2014, video, 5:25, https://www.youtube.com/watch?v=xIYX-kxeZIs.

CHAPTER 11: TAKING OFF THE TRAINING WHEELS
1. "Women and Men in the Ministry of Imago Dei Community: A Mutualist Position of Full Partnership and Shared Leadership," Imago Dei Community, http://idcpdx.com/position-change/.
2. Heather Thompson Day, "The Work Is the Platform," August 26, 2021, in Viral Jesus, *Christianity Today*, produced by Loren Joseph, podcast, https:// www.christianitytoday.com/ct/podcasts/viral-jesus/work-is-platform-karen -swallow-prior.html.

CHAPTER 13: WELCOME TO MY PITY PARTY
1. *Merriam-Webster*, s.v. "self-pity (n.)," accessed April 18, 2022, https://www
.merriam-webster.com/dictionary/self-pity.
2. Amy Morin, "9 Ways to Get Past Self-Pity: How to Stop a Downward Spiral
before It Starts," *Psychology Today*, May 8, 2015, https://www.psychologytoday
.com/us/blog/what-mentally-strong-people-dont-do
/201505/9-ways-get-past-self-pity.

CHAPTER 14: EVEN IF . . .
1. Richard J. Foster, *Celebration of Discipline: The Path to Spiritual Growth* (San
Francisco: HarperCollins, 1988), 55.

APPENDIX
1. "About Us," Be the Bridge, accessed May 5, 2022, https://bethebridge.com
/about/.

ABOUT THE AUTHOR

AMY SEIFFERT is the author of *Grace Looks Amazing on You* and is on the teaching team at Brookside Church. She is an affiliate Cru staff member and a regular YouVersion Bible teacher. She loves to travel and speak (and try new foods on all her adventures!). Amy is married to her college sweetheart, Rob, and they live in Bowling Green, Ohio, with their three kids.

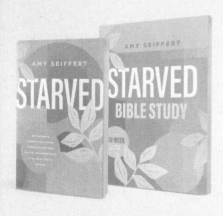